FOR
CHRIST
AND
COUNTRY

LAMBERT C. MIMS

FOR
CHRIST
AND
COUNTRY

2616

Fleming H. Revell Company
Old Tappan, New Jersey

All Scripture quotations are from the *King James Version of the Bible* unless otherwise identified.

Preface

WHEN BOYISH-LOOKING Lambert C. Mims decided to run for commissioner of historic Mobile, Alabama, the political pros smiled condescendingly and many good people were dismayed. It was pretty much agreed that it couldn't be done; a political novice just doesn't get anywhere in a race where the prize is a seat on the three-man commission which governs a thriving city.

With no previous political experience whatsoever, and with practically no previous political interest, Lambert C. Mims ran and won. Here he tells how he won Mobile's highest office, and what it's like to take God into politics.

The first time we visited this young man in his spacious offices in downtown Mobile, he spoke enthusiastically of his job. At the time, he was completing his term as public works commissioner, prior to taking over as mayor, and his responsibilities ranged from engineering and public works to maintenance of seven hundred and twenty miles of streets, along with such unromantic duties as supervision of garbage collection, refuse disposal, and sanitation.

Sanitation is no simple problem in Mobile. The city lies virtually at sea level, and when there have been heavy rains and the tide is in, there is no place for storm drainage to go. There are also the universal problems of air and water pollution.

Mayor Mims has done something very promising about pollution. When he became the youngest commissioner Mobile had ever elected, the city had been burning its refuse for forty years, creating in the process a considerable amount of mess, stench, and menace to the public health. Mims ended the burning and began converting the refuse to public profit. Now, after the thrice-weekly garbage collection, magnets remove any metal from the conglomeration, and what is left is ground up, aerated, and transformed into compost. This is dried, bagged, and sold to provide life and beauty for a good many lawns, golf courses and gardens. The compost program was begun before Mims was elected commissioner of public works, but it didn't work efficiently until he took it over.

As we talked in the city hall offices, the phone rang. The caller apparently was disturbed at the commissioner's interference with the burning of some refuse on the state docks.

"There's no earthly reason," we heard Mims say, "why the state should be burning refuse inside our city limits. We don't let anyone else do it.

"They can dump it for land fill the way they're supposed to. I'm going to *stop* that burning, even if I have to go clear to the governor."

From the way he said that, we got an idea of what makes so many people admire Lambert C. Mims.

The mayor is young and intensely committed to good government. We have the feeling that he is still at the threshold of his career, and we believe that every reader will thrill, as we have, to this account of a Christian in politics. We devoutly hope that a good many will follow his example and get seriously involved in improving their communities and their country.

The Publishers

Contents

FOR
CHRIST
AND
COUNTRY

How I Got Involved

I AM NOT A politician. Strange as it may seem, I had never taken part in any kind of political activity until I began campaigning for my present job as commissioner and mayor of my city. Never before had I enrolled with a political party, nor even carried a political sticker on my automobile. When elections came along, I knew so little about most of the candidates that I'm afraid I seldom voted very intelligently. Although I sometimes felt a little guilty because I was doing nothing to further good government, politics just didn't grab me.

Not, that is, until an unusual chain of events began to unfold in a Mobile supermarket. I was checking stock in connection with my food brokerage business when a salesman friend, Val Wilheim, came down the aisle with an unusual expression on his face.

"Lambert," he said, "you ought to run for commissioner."

The idea struck me as so preposterous that I thought Val was joking. "Yes," I laughed, "and Lassie ought to run for president."

"No," Van said, "I mean it. You know how corrupt things have been getting at City Hall. Unless there's a change soon, Mobile is going the way of the other seaport towns that wind up specializing in narcotics and venereal disease. We need men like you in public office. Please think about it."

I did think about it, briefly and pleasantly—who doesn't enjoy daydreaming now and then?—but not seriously.

A few days later I was telephoning a friend in the Baptist Brotherhood, in which I take an active part, when he suddenly suggested that I ought to get into the upcoming race for commissioner. Again I brushed the thought aside; but about a week later, when a third friend said casually that he thought I ought to run for commissioner, I suspected a plot. A careful check made clear that this was not the case. In fact, the three men were from different parts of the city and in different occupations, and none of them knew that the others had urged me to get into civic affairs.

I discussed all this with my wife, Reecie, and I wondered if perhaps God was trying to speak to me through what otherwise must be the strangest of coincidences. It was certainly true that something ought to be done about our deteriorating city government. I have no intention of pointing the finger at the administration then in power, but I think you will get an idea of the general situation if you will look at any city where the "ins" have drifted along for too long without challenge. Mobile needed better police protection, better protection against fires and flooding, and more attention to parks, playgrounds and youth programs. Instead of the new taxes that were being proposed, I was sure that the city needed less wasteful spending and the instituting of such practices as competitive-bid buying. There was no question that Mobile needed a change, but the world of politics was new to me, and, to confess the honest truth, more than a little frightening.

I tried to look at every side of the situation. I had lived in Mobile for nearly twenty years; here my wife and I had made many friends, my boys had grown up, and my business, the Mims Brokerage Company, had prospered. The people of Mobile had been good to us, and we took pride in the city's historic past.

More than a century before the pilgrims entered Plymouth harbor, a Spanish expedition sailed into Mobile Bay and named it *Bahia de Spiritu Santo*, Bay of the Holy Spirit. Fort Louis de la Mobile was established in 1702, before there was a United States of America, and Mobile is one of the oldest cities in the nation. It was Mobile Bay that Admiral Farragut was sailing into during the Civil War when he gave the famous order, "Damn the torpedoes! . . . go ahead full speed." During World Wars I and II our city contributed millions of dollars worth of ships and vital products to this nation's security. Today Mobile is one of America's leading seaports. It has been ruled by the French, British, and Spanish and also has flown the flags of the Republic of Alabama, the Confederate States, and the United States of America. The six flags that symbolize its history point to a destiny as a truly international city of the future.

I had gone to school with a boy named Tom Weatherford. He was a descendant of the Creek Indian Chief, Red Eagle or William Weatherford, who had led a night attack against Fort Mims sixty miles north of Mobile in 1813. The history of Fort Mims, founded in Alabama by Mimses who had migrated from the Carolinas, and its infamous massacre were very real to Tom and me. My ancestor, Samuel Mims, and more than five hundred men, women and children had been slaughtered in that unexpected attack. Red Eagle later surrendered to Andrew Jackson, apologized for the massacre, and was pardoned; he lived in peace and tranquility until he died a natural death. I used to tell Tom jokingly that one of these days I was going to get even with him. I took pride in the fact that the Mims

13

family had been contributing to the building of my state and country for more than one hundred fifty years.

While I plowed cotton under the hot sun on my father's upstate farm, I was often oblivious to the plodding mule and the turning soil as I dreamed of the future. I decided I was going to become somebody and have some influence in the world.

When I moved to Mobile and started my own business, I never imagined I might someday become mayor, but I came to love the city's thriving energy and its fine people. Mobile, with all its commerce and important industries, its own Mardi Gras and its thirty-five-mile azalea trail, its Senior Bowl game and Junior Miss Pageant, its gracious memories and its hopes for the future, must not fall prey to the crime and corruption which have invaded so many cities. Could it be that God wanted me to have a part in saving this great city from evil forces?

Reecie was not enthusiastic about the idea of having her husband mixed up in a political campaign. However, we both felt that we owed it to God to make the whole thing a matter of prayer.

"Lord," I prayed, "You know that I'm active in Your work. I'm witnessing for You in every way I can, and I want to do Your will. If I enter this race for commissioner of Mobile and make a bad showing, it will reflect on You and Your church. If I run, I'll just have to win. Lord, please make it clear to me what I should do. If You want me to run, I want to know it!"

I was chairman of the Board of Deacons of my church, president of the Baptist Brotherhood of Mobile, president of the local Camp of Gideons, and active in the Christian Businessmen's Committee. Everyone who knew me knew that I was a Christian, and the people who had known me before I became a Christian knew that something had happened to change my entire way of life. I dared not bring discredit on the Saviour who had changed my life. I couldn't run for public office and win an honorable mention. God's honor would be at stake; Christ's church would be on the line. If I ran, I would have to win. To make a bad showing would be a bad testimony. *I had to know what to do.*

I could picture people who weren't Christians sneering, "That guy's supposed to be a Christian leader, but the Christians didn't vote for him. What kind of leader is that? And what kind of Christians are those he thinks he's leading?"

A whole lot was at stake.

I kept on talking to the Lord, in what you might call a man-to-Man way. My wife prayed with me, and I took my problem to some special friends. These were the men in a prayer group who met together every Saturday night.

"Men," I told them, "I'm going to ask you to do something that will probably sound pretty strange. I want you to pray earnestly about a decision I have to make, probably the most important decision I've ever made. I can't tell you what it's about, but I want you to pray."

Those men prayed as I asked them to, and my pastor prayed, and I talked to the Lord day in and day out.

Gradually the answer began to come. God impressed me with the need for Christians to become involved in public affairs. He laid it on my heart that His people must come off the sidelines of life and become participants. I saw that one important area of Christian stewardship is making the world a better place, and that this could certainly be done by serving in public office.

I began to realize that I was being offered an opportunity

15

to show where I stood, and to express my Christian witness in a new way. Deep within me, I felt that God was leading me to seek a place as a commissioner. I decided to place myself in nomination.

Winning would take some doing. I belonged to no political party, and members of the commission were always backed by one of the major parties.. Furthermore, I was only thirty-five. No one that young had ever been elected commissioner in the history of Mobile.

When I told Reecie my decision, she was not surprised at all. "Honey," she said, "you're going to win. I'm sure of it."

2

Campaigning to Win

EVENTUALLY, of course, I did win the election, though at the time my chances looked very slim to many people. After I won, inquiries began to come from all over asking how I had done it. In this chapter, I want to retrace the main steps of what turned out to be one of Mobile's most exciting campaigns.

Politics was a whole new world for me, and when I started into it, I can't say that I always knew what I was doing. But I did have a pretty good idea of exactly what I would have to do to wage a successful campaign, as well as what it might cost.

Television, billboard advertising, and all the things that make a candidate known cost money. I figured that my expenses would be at least $25,000. We actually spent more than $35,000, and although this was a lot of money for a political novice to raise, it is probably infinitesimal compared to the amounts spent in many city campaigns. It costs so much to get elected to public office today that many candidates are hopelessly obligated before they begin—sold out body and soul to the people who paid the bills. I didn't intend to be obligated to anyone, and I'm pleased to say that I came through the campaign a free man. I made it clear throughout that I was not going to make any deals of any kind. When I make a decision, I want it to be based solely on what is right and best for all concerned. The fact that most of our contributions were small ones pleased me a lot more than if the whole campaign had been financed by a few large gifts.

I began to make a plan. I visualized every step I would have to take to win the election, and I blocked out on a calendar what would have to be done each week until Election Day August 17, 1965. In my heart I was as sure as Reecie was that I could and would win, but I dared not take any chances. I began to work hard, as though I would lose unless I put everything I had into the campaign. Today I can't think of anything basic we should have done that we didn't do, or anything we did that we shouldn't have. We just worked as hard as we knew how.

That "we" includes not only Reecie, but everyone in the organization we built. The man who became my campaign chairman is my brother Jeff. He is a Catholic who works just as hard in his church as I do in mine; while I was president of the Baptist Brotherhood, Jeff was president of the local Holy Name Society. Through his influence, many Catholics and Jews united behind me with the many Protestants who knew me and what I stood for. My cochairman was my best friend, Dennis Moore. We rented a campaign headquarters, where dozens of volunteers worked all day and half the night. Jeff and Dennis practically slept there. It was often two in the morning before we went home.

All our workers were volunteers. This was quite a change from the political operation where the ward heelers pay people to work. Our workers had a dedication and enthusiasm that no money could have bought. It was a fine thing for our city to have so many people involved together in this crusade for better government.

We formed a finance committee of one hundred men. Each member agreed to contact ten other men for funds and support. We also set up advertising committees, telephone committees, ward committees—every one of Mobile's thirty-eight wards was organized—and committees for various other aspects of the campaign.

Volunteers came from everywhere. Housewives who had never before been concerned with politics got on the phone, stuffed envelopes, cranked mimeograph machines, passed out campaign literature and worked for our victory. Businessmen, laborers, church members, young people and all kinds of citizens came to the front and cooperated. One man who worked extremely hard was Bobby Tillman, who had lost one leg in an automobile accident. He operates a taxi company, and he worked like a Trojan. A Greek gentleman, Manuel Clikas, who also worked very hard, was about the only person in our whole organization who had had any experience in campaigning. He was perfect on the telephone; he and many other workers called everyone they knew or could think of. Countless hours of time were donated by hundreds of people who expected only one thing in return—good government.

We arranged for six weeks of meetings at one of Mobile's finest motor hotels and restaurants. Each week about forty persons from all walks of life—doctors, lawyers, dentists, businessmen, truck drivers, factory workers, farmers, members of churches and of civic clubs—were invited to come and hear about our program. I explained to these people why I was running for office, what I was concerned about, and what I proposed to do toward reasonable, clean government in our city. The response was terrific. Most of those present enthusiastically pledged their support, and week after week, as new groups came, the results were multiplied.

All over Mobile women opened their homes for afternoon teas. They made cakes and cookies, served tea and coffee, and invited their friends in to meet me. I would usually spend thirty minutes at one of these teas, chatting informally and presenting my program, and then I'd drive on to the next place.

When people think of political rallies, they usually think of a lot of noise, drinking and ballyhoo. Our organizational rallies were altogether different. We generally had a piano and a song director present, and we would open the rally with some singing, starting with "America" or our national anthem; then we went right into our business, bringing everyone up to date on what had happened and filling them in on what we wanted them to do in the next few days before we had our next meeting. After that we had a time for fellowship and refreshments. The drinks were coffee or soda, and we ate cake and dessert brought by the ladies. Everyone thoroughly enjoyed the whole thing. Lasting friendships were made at our gatherings; people who had never met before have become very dear friends as a result. The whole campaign had very healthy results for the Mobile community.

A political unknown was getting organized. An independent candidate, never heard of in most political circles, was laying the groundwork for what was to become, according to some observers familiar with local politics, one of the finest campaign organizations this area has seen.

Everything had been planned and we worked the plan. We purchased television time, radio time, newspaper space, billboard advertising and campaign literature. We didn't even have an advertising agency; I was my own advertising manager. We laid out every one of our ads and circulars ourselves. In all our ads we used the same simple appeals and the same general motif. Day-glo lettering in orange and black blanketed billboards and auto bumpers; the public could hardly ignore admonitions like these: RETURN REASON TO CITY HALL. VOTE MIMS. ELECT A BUSINESSMAN TO PLACE THREE, MOBILE CITY COMMISSION.

Some mornings I got up at three or four o'clock to meet the early shifts of the men in Mobile's factories and other places of business. Our city is served by four railroads, four major airlines, and one hundred steamship lines. We have a three million bushel grain elevator, a gypsum company, two paper mills, and a number of chemical plants. Mobile workers build and repair ships, refine oil, fabricate metal, and produce iron, steel, aluminum, cement, roofing, wood pulp, paper products, clothing, and bakery products. I wanted as many of these men and women as possible to know of my interest in better government. I shook hands with them, passed out my circulars, and asked them for their votes.

Funds came in, a little here and a little there. A Catholic priest (now deceased) contributed twenty-five dollars. We accepted every contribution offered, no matter how small it might be. Once a man has given you a dollar, you've got his support.

About thirty autos carried Mims campaign signs. To keep our opposition guessing about where I was and what I might be doing, I often switched cars with friends. One day I was driving a Pontiac, the next a Chevrolet, and the next a Ford or a Chrysler.

We prayed and we worked. As the days and weeks passed and we followed the steps on our campaign calendar, a tremendous feeling of good will and enthusiasm developed. People who had never before had any real interest in politics worked day and night with a common purpose. All of us had a good time as we looked forward to Election Day.

Thousands of citizens became interested. As the election drew near, the city was blanketed with brochures. Every weekend we visited every shopping center, and we saw that a piece of literature was placed under the windshield wiper of every parked car. We distributed bumper stickers and bought hundreds of inches of newspaper space. I made countless personal appearances and radio announcements, and dozens of television appeals.

It was on television that the campaign was really won. I wasn't able to pre-record my TV appearances as my opponents had, but this gave me an unusual advantage. Years of sales and church work gave me the ability, not only to speak with assurance into a live television camera, but also an interesting additional opportunity. I was able to tie the day's events into what I said each evening, and, according to my co-workers, I came across better than my opponents whose previously recorded statements looked canned because they were.

When they look into a television, many people seem to freeze. I didn't. I thought of all the people out there all over Mobile, more than 230,000 of them, looking and listening. They were people who needed a change for the better in their political leaders, and I threw my heart into letting them see that here was one candidate who really intended to work for their best interests. I believe the main thing in television work is the same as in all communication—to be able to reach people, understand them, and talk to them from the heart. You must mean what you say. People can tell whether you're sincere or a phony. If you want to convince them, you had better believe what you're telling them.

When Election Day arrived, we knew that we had done our best. That morning, Reecie and our two sons and I met at breakfast with a sense that everything was now in the hands of the Lord. We turned the whole matter over to Him. I prayed that He would go behind the curtains with the voters and direct their hands to pull the right levers. I asked for victory if it was His will that I be elected and if this would glorify Him. If my election would not glorify His name, I prayed for the grace to accept defeat like a Christian.

That night an expectant group gathered at our campaign headquarters. Our workers began phoning in the results as soon as the polls closed, at 6 P.M. There was an air of tremendous excitement all through the evening. All the telephones at our headquarters were in constant use as our workers at that end totaled the votes. A television set had been brought in, and people were milling around with portable radios.

When the votes swept in from our downtown Mobile area, a good many of those present became pretty glum, for the majority were voting along traditional party lines. Another group, the silk stocking group which consists of the wealthier and older aristocratic families of Mobile, gave most of its votes to an opponent whose father had once been mayor.

The suburban wards were the last to report. Now the tide definitely turned. My strength came from the suburbs, as Kennedy's did in 1960 and Nixon's in 1968. The younger voters, parents raising families and people who had moved to Mobile from other cities, gave me their votes. We had a clear majority. All that handshaking in the suburban areas of Mobile had paid off.

The television cameras zoomed toward me as reporters

and media interviewers all tried to ask questions at once. "Now that you have emerged victorious from this hard-fought campaign," asked a television announcer, "what word do you have for the people of Mobile?"

Turning toward the cameras, I thanked the people for their confidence in me. I thanked those who had worked so hard to make the campaign a success. I thought of my mother and father, who had been anxiously awaiting the results as they sat by their television set on the farm where I had grown up.

"Mother and Dad," I said, "I want you to pray for me as I undertake this new task at City Hall. I'm a long way from the cotton patch tonight."

3

No Bed of Roses

I SHALL NEVER forget my first day in the historic City Hall of Mobile, with the excitement, the anxiety, and the realization of the responsibility I was assuming in my new position as a public official. Telephones were ringing, department heads were standing in line to see the new commissioner of public works, and flowers kept arriving until my office looked more like a florist's shop than a public official's office. Friends and associates came in to pay me a sort of inaugural visit, and many telegrams wished me success in my new undertaking. To say that I was nervous would be putting it mildly!

Amid all the excitement, a package arrived. Having no idea what it might contain, I opened it slowly and very cautiously. I carefully removed the outer layer of wrapping paper, then the cover of a box, then an inner wrapper. My eyes fell on one of the most beautiful Bibles I have ever seen. It was handsomely bound in red leather. Inside the front cover I read:

> Presented to Commissioner Lambert C. Mims on the day of his inauguration, October 4, 1965, by the Mobile Baptist Association.

Tears welled up in my eyes. Amazed and overwhelmed, I bowed my head in humility as my hands gripped this beautifully bound copy of God's Word and I thanked Him for the confidence that the Baptists of Mobile had in me and for the love expressed in this presentation. The first of many prayers that have been uttered in this office was lifted up that day as I asked God to bless me and use me and keep me ever close to Him.

That night, when the inaugural ceremonies were held at the Municipal Auditorium, the new red Bible was proudly taken to this very meaningful event. Several hundred citizens of Mobile, along with the families of the three newly elected commissioners, were present. After the preliminaries were taken care of and the speeches made, Judge John L. Moore, the probate judge of Mobile County, used my new Bible to administer the oath of office to each commissioner.

The red leather Bible was taken back to my office and placed on a corner of my desk, where it has been in evidence ever since as a testimony to God and a witness that I trust Him for wisdom, courage and strength. It has been used on many occasions, especially as I have counseled with people who have come to me with spiritual problems. During visits to my office about various matters, individuals have picked up the "Inaugural Bible" and have read from it as I breathed a prayer that God would speak to them through it.

Of course, all kinds of things can and do happen in an office like mine. Early in my new career, a newspaper reporter wrote that I was finding my new job "no bed of roses." He was right. I never expected that becoming commissioner and then mayor *would* be a bed of roses, but I have found that the problems are often thornier than I could have imagined.

People come to the mayor for all kinds of things which are far beyond my sphere of authority. One noon while I was eating lunch with a friend in a local restaurant, a lady stopped at our table and spoke.

"Mayor Mims," she said, "we've just got to get one of those iron lungs in the Providence Hospital." (This is one of Mobile's fine private hospitals.) "Won't you see that one is installed there right away?"

The fact is that I have no more authority than the mayor of Hong Kong to add to the equipment of a private institution such as the one she named.

One day the telephone in my office rang and an angry female voice exploded into my ear. "Mayor, there's a dead dog under my house and I want you to get it out before the smell drives me out of my mind. So far your men have refused to touch it. When are you going to take care of it?"

"Lady," I said, "you know we can't go on your property. Our city employees have been carefully instructed to stay off private property at all times. We just cannot do things of this nature."

"Mr. Mims," the lady said indignantly, "I thought you were a Christian."

"I am a Christian," I said. "What's that got to do with a dead dog?"

"Well, if you were a Christian you'd send someone down here to go under this house and get that dog!"

It took some time for me to convince my caller that I could not legally do what she wanted, and that she was wrong in thinking I could. I explained that if she would have the dead animal removed and placed on the curb according to city regulations, my men would remove it. Finally the lady apologized for what she had said and hung up.

Although my work as a public official is more satisfying than anything I have ever done, except leading someone to faith in Christ, it is also one of the hardest jobs I can think of. I believe it's the most difficult political job in the state. No one expects to get his senator or his governor on the phone immediately, whenever he has a problem, but anyone in Mobile can pick up his telephone almost any time of the day or night and call me. And he expects me to answer personally, and help him out with whatever may be bothering him.

I get hundreds of requests from people who want me to do something. My telephone is ringing constantly. Fortunately, my secretary, Mrs. Melva Regan, who is very efficient, is able to handle many of the calls and refers many others to people who can handle them. Often, too, people are practically standing in line waiting to see me. I try to talk to as many of them as I can. Very often, I have the opportunity not only to help them with problems relating to the city, but also to witness to what Christ means to me.

Sometimes a taxpayer will phone me sounding as angry as a wet hen, shouting or screaming. I usually let such a caller go on for awhile; then I stop him and say, "There's no need to shout like that." After a person calms down, he's more likely to listen to reason.

Some days we get more complaints than others. When you have to deal with a couple of unreasonable people it may spoil nearly the whole day. Fortunately, most people are sensible and appreciative when things are done as they should be. Sometimes I get irritated or frustrated, but then I have to get hold of myself and try to realize that *every* day isn't this bad. My job can be hard and hectic, but I love people and I get a lot of satisfaction from doing my best to help them.

Everyone's problem is the most important in the world to him, no matter how small it may look to someone else. The collector didn't pick up Mr. Jones' garbage, or Mrs. Smith's garbage can is bent, or there's a pot hole like the Grand Canyon in front of the Brown house (according to Mr. Brown). The weeds need cutting in the city lot near

Mrs Green or Mrs. Johnson wants a street light in her block. Usually it's this kind of thing that people phone me about. To the person troubled with it, his problem is very important, and he expects me to drop everything else until that problem is settled.

Of course, I try to serve the people of my city to the best of my ability, and I expect all the employees in the city government to have the same attitude. When I took office I found that many of the city workers were slow to respond to the citizens' just requests. They seemed to be dragging their feet much of the time, taking the attitude, "What's the use?" Things that should have been done promptly were often put aside, forgotten, or done only half way.

Early in my first week as commissioner of public works, I went out with one of my supervisors to see how his department was running. While the two of us were having a cup of coffee, a man who looked like a laborer approached my associate about a matter which had evidently been neglected for some time. The man said, "I'm a taxpayer. I want this taken care of."

The supervisor reached in his pocket and pulled out a nickel. "Here's your tax," he said.

That was the kind of attitude this official had. I had to have a real heart-to-heart talk with him. "Man," I said, "I want everyone in public works to remember that the taxpayer is boss. Some people may be unreasonable, and we're not here to do more for one than for another, or to be mistreated. But no one deserves a job unless he's producing, and that goes for public office as much as for private enterprise. The taxpayers are paying your salary and mine, and let's not forget it. The minute we stop serving them the best we know how, we don't deserve our jobs."

I think I got the point across, and I started another

campaign to remind all my department heads and the men under them that we hold our jobs for one reason—to serve the people who pay our salaries. No one in public office should take the attitude that he's riding a gravy train.

Some politicians seem to be interested in people's problems only when they are campaigning. Once in office, they are no more interested in the needs of the people who elected them. That is dead wrong. When a person has a problem that something can be done about, I try my best to solve it. Whether it's a matter of street lighting or road maintenance or something else, I try to work it out to his satisfaction right away. People appreciate it when they know they don't have to keep hounding City Hall to get something done. Of course, sometimes it takes a while to get a project under way, but many problems take hardly any time to solve. The city employees of Mobile know that when there is a complaint, they are supposed to get right on it.

Personally, I get tremendous satisfaction at the end of each day in which I have served my Master and my fellow men to the best of my ability. I can't think of a more wonderful way to go to bed than with the thought, "I've done my best today to be an example *For Christ and Country.* "From the time Christ took over my life, I have never had the idea that we can rightly goof off from our opportunities and responsibilities. As a public official, I enjoy helping people, putting my best efforts into good government to redeem the time God gives me.

So although serving on the Board of Commissioners of the city of Mobile is no bed of roses, I wouldn't exchange it for any other in the world—for I feel that I am where God wants me at this time.

4

Pollution Problem Number One

As COMMISSIONER of public works I am responsible for sanitation, drainage, refuse disposal, and pollution control. My department collects garbage three times a week from nearly sixty thousand homes, and we convert much of the city's refuse into compost which we market under the trade name Mobile-Aid. If these men were not ceaselessly on the job, Mobile would soon be so swamped with refuse of all kinds that an epidemic might break out.

Most cities today have a growing problem with air pollution. When certain atmospheric conditions prevail over large cities, hundreds of deaths may result from the effect of smog on weak hearts and constitutions; the people are trapped in their city's own fumes and smoke, until these are dispersed by winds. Here in Mobile, we have found that fires often break out at dumping areas from spontaneous combustion, and we are taking precautions to eliminate these fires to prevent their polluting our atmosphere. Our industries are spending millions of dollars in this area. The control of air pollution should be one of our nation's most urgent priorities within the next decade.

Another major urban problem is water pollution. A few years ago Miami found so much foam in its drinking water that detergents were banned in several areas. Sewage and other pollution in coastal areas have produced dangerous

31

outbreaks of hepatitis, while industrial waste and pesticides have ruined rivers and lakes throughout the world. Mobile has spent more than any other city of comparable size on sewage disposal. We intend to continue fighting water pollution in the Mobile area as vigorously as any other evil.

The worst pollution problem today, however, is the pollution of the minds of the young, and indeed of all our citizens. Air and water pollution endanger people's physical health, and to the extent of my ability, I intend to keep such contamination at a minimum in Mobile. Bad as these forms of pollution are, America's Number One pollution problem, moral pollution, is completely ignored by many people who are in a position to know better. Moral pollution contaminates a person's mind and heart and endangers his eternal welfare. As a commissioner and as mayor of Mobile, I have had to take a stand against this most dangerous pollution of all.

One day I received a letter with a New Jersey postmark offering over two hundred colored pictures of nude men and women in the act of sexual intercourse. Soon afterward, my son Dale, then sixteen years old, received an identical offer in the mail. We turned these solicitations over to the postal authorities, and we urge others to do the same thing. I have asked our city attorney to determine what can be done to prevent such mailings. We are exploring the possibility of taking legal action against firms which brazenly peddle such pornography.

There is also the flood of filthy magazines and paperback books on sale in many shops and newsstands. In many cities anyone of any age can examine, read and purchase all kinds of pornographic materials.

Through a series of recent decisions, the Supreme Court has invalidated a number of state and local laws setting standards of obscenity. However, many of the decisions recognized the need for protecting young persons from pornography, and federal courts have recognized as a valid exercise of police power the prevention of certain material from being distributed to minors.

I introduced an ordinance to our board of commissioners, patterned after a New York ordinance which the Supreme Court had upheld, making it unlawful to sell or exhibit to anyone under seventeen, materials deemed harmful to minors. The ordinance covered nude, pornographic or sadistic pictures, sculpture, books, magazines or recordings. It defined nudity, sexual conduct, and sadomasochistic abuse in some detail, and nailed down standards which will be hard for anyone who wants to make a profit from filth to break. The board of commissioners enacted the ordinance on October 15, 1968.

Tremendous support for this ordinance has been evident from many Catholics; the local chapter of the Knights of Columbus commended me for my stand. I also received the backing of the Holy Name societies, the ministerial associations, and the Baptist pastors' conferences of our area.

We are getting results. One local book store operator has been sentenced to six months in jail plus a five hundred dollar fine for selling obscene materials. Another is awaiting trial following a raid which resulted in the confiscation of more than 2,500 dirty books.

Soon after I became mayor, students of the University of South Alabama produced the play *American Hurrah* in the Mobile Municipal Park. The next morning a city newspaper described this play as pointlessly vulgar. That morning my phone nearly rang off the hook as local citizens expressed their disapproval, so I called the University president, Dr. Frederick Whidden, and he promised to check into the matter.

That night Police Commissioner Arthur Outlaw, City Attorney Fred Collins, Captain Charles Wimberley (the head of our police Vice Squad) and I went to see *America Hurrah.* In our opinion, and in the opinion of many others, it was terrible—sacreligious, obscene, and without any kind of redeeming value.

The play was supposed to be shocking and to show what is going on in our country. It was certainly shocking enough. In the last act a man and a woman wearing large grotesque paper masks over their heads entered a motel room. The two began undressing and making love with all sorts of gyrations. The woman went into the washroom to finish undressing and threw the toilet seat out into the room before she emerged in a flimsy nightgown. The two tore all the pictures off the walls, pulled out the dresser drawers and threw them on the floor, and broke up the furniture. They threw their luggage on the bed, knocked the mattress and springs down inside, and tore open the pillows, scattering feathers all over the room. They found a Gideon Bible and tore it into a thousand pieces, throwing the empty covers at the wall. They drew pictures of nude women on walls and wrote four letter obscenities two feet high. Finally this nearly nude pair ran through the aisles to the rear of the theater.

We ordered the play closed. A few liberals were quick to criticize. Some protested by phone, some on radio call-in programs. I was accused of tampering with freedom of speech, of trying to regulate morals, and so on. But letters of approval poured in, too, from all over the world.

I still feel exactly as I expressed it at the time, *America Hurrah* is filth, pure and simple, and I think that it is a shame that Alabama taxpayers' money has been used to produce such degrading trash."

Lest anyone think that this incident represents some kind of deep-South provincialism, let me point out that similar crudities have produced similar responses in various parts of the United States. In a university town in Connecticut, for instance, the cast of a modern play stripped down to nearly nothing and persuaded some of the audience to strip completely. When this motley crowd started out of the theater and down the street, police arrested them. Early in 1969 ten men and women appeared nude in a play at a university town in Michigan. Police arrested them.

Several years ago, an Alabama politician tried unsuccessfully to bring dog racing into our state and city. Recently he tried again. He and others argued that we must compete for tourists with cities like Pensacola, Florida, only sixty miles away, which has long had such races. They said that dog racing would attract more conventions, bring in more revenue from extra taxes, give visitors something to do, and so on. I'm sure you have heard all these tired old arguments in your own area on behalf of some form of gambling, for, of course, gambling was the real purpose.

I opposed the whole thing unequivocally. I launched a drive against dog racing, and we gathered together the largest group ever to appear before a legislative delegation in Alabama's history. More than a thousand people came to a rally in the Municipal Auditorium. I spoke, pointing out that gambling, crime and prostitution go hand in hand. Of each dollar bet on dog racing, it was admitted that the government would get only seven cents. The fact is, I noted, gambling would cost the taxpayers much more in crime, taxes, and other losses than they would ever get out of it.

Because of the cooperation of people with common sense and Christian convictions, the drive to legalize dog racing came to a screeching halt.

There are still people who argue for gambling and say, "You've got to have something for people to *do.*" It's possible to find plenty to do without betting on races. We get along fine without it. We are attracting tourists and conventions to our city, and I don't think we need dog racing, prostitution, or the Mafia.

The current trend in movies concerns many of us. The daughter of one public official called him the meanest man in town because he refused to let her see a film in which a married woman seduced the young man who was courting her daughter. Motion pictures have become so sex-centered that it is difficult to find one that is wholesome and decent.

For a time Mobile prohibited anyone under eighteen years of age from attending a motion picture advertised as "adult," and then our local theaters made a proposal which we accepted.

After several conferences with the motion picture operators and owners, we agreed to consider their plan for improving the cinema situation. Their proposal involved rating each movie on the basis of a composite of the reports of the National Congress of Parents and Teachers, the Schools' Motion Picture Committee, the American Library Association, the General Federation of Women's Clubs, and other interested groups. Ratings varied from "adult" or "children" to "general audience." The ratings were to be advertised and the theater owners promised to seek to police the ratings. Later a similar set of ratings was adopted throughout the nation.

I discussed the proposal with Fred Collins, our city attorney, and with a number of concerned parents and clergymen. Everyone felt that this was a step in the right direction, and as mayor, I accepted it, believing the proposal was offered in good faith and in a sincere spirit of cooperation. The new system cleaned up our motion pictures considerably.

Even so, in December, 1968, there was considerable controversy in the Mobile area over the motion picture *The Fox*. This reportedly deals with two women in a lesbian relationship and depicts not only nudity but even masturbation. Several other states had taken action to prevent its being shown, and when it was announced that this film was going to begin a lengthy run in Mobile, I asked Police Commissioner Outlaw and several other city officials to attend a private viewing. I did not see it myself as I did not want to create the impression I was becoming some sort of czar or dictator because of my personal likes or dislikes. I was content to trust the judgment of others.

The judgment of these men was that *The Fox* was suggestive and filthy and that if it should be shown publicly, criminal charges should be pressed against the theater officials, in line with our anti-obscenity ordinances. Our ordinance protecting minors from pornography had not included motion pictures, since the theater owners had agreed to do everything in their power to prevent those under eighteen from attending objectionable pictures. On December 3, we amended this ordinance to include motion pictures. We also seized a print of *The Fox* and initiated criminal prosecution against the a theater group which was determined to show this film. Thereupon the theater group petitioned for a court order to restrain the city of Mobile from interfering with its plans, pleading that it would lose money and be deprived of its constitutional rights.

Circuit Judge Roy Mayhall viewed the film himself, listened to the arguments of both the city and the theater group, and announced his ruling. Stating that his verdict was not based on his personal feelings but on Supreme Court decisions, he ruled that the showing of *The Fox* must not be prohibited. "You can't legislate the morals of people," he said. Within an hour after his ruling, such long lines began to form in front of the theater that it was shown twice the first night instead of once as originally planned.

After this decision, City Attorney Fred Collins announced that he would appeal to the Alabama Supreme Court. When that court upheld the decision of the circuit court, we observed a day of mourning in Mobile. All flags on municipal buildings were flown at half-mast, and some of our citizens did the same with flags at their homes. It was my intention to make as many people as possible aware of the fact that the city of Mobile had been unable to enforce its valid ordinances. I held a press conference announcing the beginning of a vigorous campaign against the pornography peddlers. I called on all concerned Mobilians to exert every effort to keep purveyors of trash and pornography from destroying our fine community standards. I warned, "It is not an easy task, for we are battling big money. The filth racket is a multi-million-dollar operation, and it will not be easily discouraged."

I also referred to the courts which had impeded our attempts to protect our young people by saying, "It is a sad and serious thing when a community cannot regulate its own affairs and enforce its own valid and uncontested laws." I appealed to parents of all men and women of good will, "For the sake of our young people, please join this effort. With your help we will keep our moral standards high, and we will continue to have a city of which we can all be proud."

The newspapers described this as opening a war against smut. That's the kind of war I intend to continue, as long as God gives me the strength.

5

Law, Order, and God

DURING THE PAST few years in hundreds of American cities there has been a sickening welter of chaos, destruction and anarchy. Thousands of people have been injured, dozens have been killed, and hundreds of millions of dollars worth of property have gone up in smoke. No longer can we sing,

> O beautiful for patriot dream
> That sees beyond the years
> Thine alabaster cities gleam
> Undimmed by human tears!

> Katherine Lee Bates

Instead we must say with broken hearts, "Yonder in the setting sun lie the smouldering towns, torn by rioters and looters, smothering in ruin, while those responsible for such dastardly devastation are applauded like heroes." No longer does one walk the streets with a feeling of security. In many of our cities God-fearing decent citizens are afraid to come from behind locked doors, fearful that around the first corner waits some violator of law and order. Even our nation's capital has become a paradise for hoodlums and lawbreakers.

I agree with *U. S. News and World Report* (August 7, 1967) that there is a growing threat to the cities of America. That magazine stated recently that anarchy "is seen by law-enforcement experts to lie just below the surface of many of America's big cities—ready to burst into the open at the slightest provocation.

"In city after city where chaos has taken over in recent years, from New York to Birmingham to Los Angeles, the tendency has been to blame everything on 'ghettoes' or police or lack of jobs or simply hot weather.

"Yet arson, gunfire, and looting reached their real climax in Detroit—a city in a state where people are proud of their race relations."

No government has the right to look the other way when its laws are broken or its authority is questioned. One day while I was taking an out-of-town guest to his motel, my car radio started crackling and I heard one of our supervisors asking his boss what to do. This man's workers refused to pick up the leaves they were supposed to be collecting from the streets; they complained that the bundles were too heavy. Knowing that this was not the case, I cut in on the conversation and told the supervisor, "You tell the men to pick up those leaves."

I try to make decisions that are fair and right. Some of them may be wrong, but they must be obeyed until I am overruled or retired by the voters. No organization, and certainly no government, can function unless it is built on justice, hope and respect for authority.

Charles S. Hyneman, formerly a president of the American Political Science Association and now professor of government at Indiana University, has stated:

We have fallen into a mood of acceptance of "protest" as being good in itself. Because the Negro has a just cause, it is assumed disorders he creates should be excused no matter the extent of disruption to a city or even a nation. Ordinary duties of citizenship are supposed not to apply to him.

Obviously, this is disastrous. A society cannot be peaceful and productive when there is continuing civil strife and turmoil. It can exist for a time in a constant state of civil turmoil, but the outcome of this is an authoritarian regime which imposes discipline by repression.

My own city of Mobile has seen much tension. During two provocative marches, thousands of dollars had to be spent in police protection, and other incidents have cost our taxpayers hundreds of thousands of dollars along with untold hours of anxiety and anguish. Small minorities here and elsewhere are causing diturbances that could erupt into holocausts at the drop of a hat and literally destroy the heart of many American cities. We in the government of Mobile have made it clear that we intend to enforce the law and keep order. We have instructed our police to use any measure necessary to stop anyone throwing firebombs, looting or the like unless the law violator ceases immediately. If an arsonist or rioter will not stop his criminal activity, he must be stopped, even if he has to be shot. This is the only way we know how to maintain law and order.

The notorious Detroit riot of 1967, in which 41 people were killed, 2,250 injured, and 4,000 arrested, began when police raided a speakeasy in an area of hippies and prostitutes. Residents started throwing bricks and stones at the police, smashing the window in a police cruiser. Right there, in the opinion of *Newsweek* (August 7, 1967), the authorities made their initial fatal mistake. Instead of moving forward "in full force to nip the trouble in the bud," they followed a "walk-soft" strategy and decided "to show the flag but made no effort to beat back the crowd—a decision bitterly denounced by whites and Negro moderates alike in the aftermath." Then, as crowds began looting and burning police did little but open swimming pools and hope for the best. Only when it was too late did the city police, the state troopers, and the National Guard act decisively, and by then things were so far out of control that paratroopers had to be flown in from Kentucky and North Carolina.

A government has no right to turn its back on those who would destroy a city or take people's property. The only way to save a city is to mainain the law. Mobile has a special police detail that operates at night, staking out places that are likely to be robbed. This detail observed two men enter a store and emerge with a bag of money. When the men were told to halt, one of them wheeled with a gun. Unfortunately, he was killed. But if those who violate the law will not stop when they are so instructed, there's no alternative. He must be shot.

We need a new respect for private property. In a day when we hear of many other rights, this fundamental one must not be forgotten. Abraham Lincoln put this well when he said:

> Property is the fruit of labor, property is desirable; it is a positive good in the world. That some should be rich shows that others may become rich, and hence is just encouragement to industry and enterprise.
>
> Let not him who is houseless pull down the house of another, but let him work diligently and build one for himself, thus by example assuringthat his own shall be safe from violence when built.

There is too much permissiveness in America today. Often the courts respond to clear violations of the law with no punishment, or with such a light fine that the violators are encouraged to repeat the same offense. One man convicted of entering a place of business and trying to remove the safe was given a suspended sentence of six months. This simply encouages crime. When I was a boy, people were afraid of the penitentiary and the electric chair, and they thought twice before they broke into a man's home or held up someone on the street. In those days men knew that pay day was coming when laws were broken. Today there is little fear left.

Permissiveness is all through our society. Too many parents do not seem to know or care what their children are doing, nor guide them into respect for others, for property, or for God. When I did something wrong as a boy, my Daddy set me right with a belt or a hickory stick. I've never forgotten his lessons in right and wrong, and I never will forget them.

There are many broken homes as a result of some 400,000 divorces every year, and there is a move to make divorce even easier! Millions of young people are being brought up without either a mother or a father of their own, and millions more with no moral training whatever. It is not surprising that many of these youngsters grow up to become criminals. Children don't have to be taught to do wrong. They have that nature from the old Adam in them; they do wrong automatically, unless there is very strong guidance toward God and what is right.

Discipline is necessary in the schools. I understand that many of the old-fashioned forms of punishment are illegal in many schools today. When I was in high school, and that was not too many years ago, if a boy misbehaved the principal would take him into his office and let him feel a paddle.I don't think too many criminals have come out of that little country high school.

We have militant groups in Mobile who would like to throw fire bombs and tear up the town, but we don't intend to allow this.

In the fall of 1968 I learned that students at the University of Alabama, at Tuscaloosa, were planning to invite as speakers Eldredge Cleaver of the Black Panthers, Herbert Aptheker of the Communist Party, Mark Rudd of the Students for a Democratic Society, and Jerry Rubin, leader of the Yippies.

Cleaver's racist extremism is notorious. He had said in San Francisco only a few weeks previously:

> America is up against the wall. This whole apparatus, this capitalistic system and its institutions and police . . . all need to be assigned to the garbage can of history. . . . If we can't have it, nobody's gonna have it. . . . We need lawyers today who have a law book in one hand and a gun in the other. . . . I hope you'll take your guns and shoot judges and police.

The activities of Aptheker and of Rudd, who have instigated so many student revolts at universities, are well known. Rubin's Yippies disgusted many people at the 1968 convention of the Democratic Party in Chicago, as they labelled the presidential candidates "pigs," practiced free love in Lincoln Park, and threw rocks, ash trays and feces at police. Yippie demands included withdrawal of all American troops from foreign soil, abolition of the draft, disarming the police, abolishing money, freedom from the drudgery of work, and legalization of marijuana and all other psychedelic drugs.

I believe in free speech, but not in license for men like these to try to overthrow our American institutions. I sent the following telegram to Dr. Frank Rose, presidentof the University of Alabama, and to Governor Albert Brewer.

PLEASE IN THE NAME OF ALL THAT IS RIGHT TAKE IM-
MEDIATE STEPS TO PROHIBIT BLACK PANTHER LEADER EL-
DREDGE CLEAVER, YIPPIE JERRY RUBIN, COMMUNIST
HERBERT APTHEKER AND OTHER UN-AMERICAN CHARAC-
TERS FROM APPEARING ON THE CAMPUS OF ONE OF AMERI-
CA'S GREATEST UNIVERSITIES.

IT'S HIGH TIME IN A DAY WHEN IT SEEMS THAT EVERY-
THING GOES IN THE NAME OF ACADEMIC FREEDOM OR FREE-
DOM OF SPEECH, FOR MEN IN HIGH PLACES TO STAND FIRM
AGAINST THOSE WHO WOULD WANT US DIVIDED AND DE-
STROYED.

The governor and Dr. Rose answered, pledging that
they would not allow these men to speak on the campus.
They were denied this privilege and never came to Alabama.

Luther W. Youngdahl has said, "The freedom of American society is an ordered freedom, a freedom under God
and under the law." The first responsibility of the citizen
is to abide by the laws of this country. If a law is unjust,
it may be legally contested and repealed in accordance
with the provisions in our Constitution and our legal system. Responsible citizens take advantage of this privilege
rather than take to the streets. If a small minority of militant, irresponsible, lawless individuals has free reign in the
streets to do as it pleases whenever it disagrees with the
majority, our government must fall apart.

This country was founded by godly, responsible men.
The molders of our great Republic were men with the
conviction that citizenship requires responsibility. They
shed their sweat and their blood to establish a land of laws.
Today we need men who are responsible enough to want
right rather than riot, to respect the law rather than resort

46

to looting, to realize that they are debtors rather than to become detractors.

Truly we are debtors to the gallant, God-fearing men and women of the *Mayflower*. We are debtors to those who fearlessly carved this nation out of a wilderness, to the framers of our Constitution, to those who have served us well in places of leadership, to those who have given their very lives that we might be free, and to those who now defend us in the service of their country. We are debtors indeed.

The true citizen is conscious of the great price that has been paid for our freedom, and is willing to do anything within the framework of law to keep it and pass it on to his children.

The thousands of dollars which often have to be spent for police protection could be used to better advantage in training programs for the poor, jobs for the unemployed, and public improvements. Public marches and protests accomplish absolutely nothing that could not be accomplished better by reasonable men at the conference table. The millions which have been lost in violence in this country, and in protection of the public from marchers and demonstrators, could have fed multitudes of hungry people and might have helped our nation forward instead of subjecting it to world ridicule.

Law-breaking and disorder are often excused on the grounds of alleged police brutality. The following letter from a Christian mother to the police department of a large city in Texas presents this subject from a perspective to which I hope many people will give serious thought.

Dear Sirs:

One of the most common phrases heard in our society

and our city today is "police brutality." Perhaps I don't understand the meaning, but I would like to give you one mother's viewpoint on this subject.

To begin, I should first tell you that I have two teen-age sons, and being a mother I cannot help but want the very best of everything for them. I am a "typical mother" in that I don't want to see them hurt by anyone. I am not a typical mother, for I see things many mothers never hear of, much less become involved in, because my husband is a minister and we see the very best and the sordid worst.

I would like you to be *brutal* with my sons. Is that a surprise?

If you find them speeding in a car, PLEASE BE BRUTAL. I have sat at the hospital holding a grieving mother's hand because of someone's mistake. That was *brutal.* I have gone with my husband to tell a wife her husband was killed. That was *brutal.* I have helped nurse a beautiful teen-age girl crippled in a wreck. That was *brutal.* I have played organ music at funeral services for babies, teen-agers, and adults because someone drove too fast. That was *brutal.*

If you should catch my under-age sons with liquor in their possession, PLEASE BE BRUTAL. I have sat all night by my husband's side trying to help piece together two under-age young men's lives, both broken by drinking. That was *brutal.* I have listened to the horrors experienced by another man while he was drunk and heard him recall the many jails he had served time in for this. That was *brutal.* I have helped feed hungry children because a drunken father didn't come home. That was *brutal.* I have tried to console a mother whose daughter was killed after being struck by a drunken driver. That was *brutal.*

If you should find my sons with drugs in their possession, PLEASE BE BRUTAL! I have tried to help rehabilitate a woman just out of prison for shooting her husband while she was drugged. That was *brutal*. I have seen a handsome young man turn into an old ugly one because of drugs. That was *brutal*. I have seen a young mother who was addicted to a drug scream and rave for lack of a "fix." That was *brutal*.

If you find my sons committing any kind of immoral act or carrying any pornographic materials, PLEASE BE BRUTAL! I have listened to the sad cry of a young girl who was pregnant but not married. That was *brutal*. I have been present when a boy and girl broke the news to their parents that they had to marry. That was *brutal*. I have seen a lovely expensive home and yard completely torn up by vandals. That was *brutal*. I have wiped a little boy's tears and helped him hunt for his stolen bicycle. That was *brutal*.

If you should ever catch my sons doing anything illegal PLEASE BE BRUTAL! I have come to realize that your kind of "brutality" cannot in any way compare with the brutality that comes from breaking our laws. My husband and I have tried to teach our sons that their rights end where someone else's begin. We believe they have learned this lesson, but in any case they forget, we look to you and others who influence their lives—teachers, coaches, etc.— to see that they remember. And if you must be brutal to remind them —THEN PLEASE, BE BRUTAL! I do not want my two sons to grow into two grown-up boys. I want them to become men, able to assume their places in this world and make a good contribution to it. I sincerely hope they won't need your help, but if they do, and if you must, THEN BE BRUTAL!

One of the best analysis of riots and lawlessness which I have seen was made by a young lawyer only twenty-eight years old. Having served in the armed forces, he had a special appreciation of the majesty of the law, and rightly he was concerned about the number of people who were putting themselves above the law of the land. Referring to the increasing tendency of certain individuals to take the law into their own hands with total disregard for the rights of others, he said:

By such examples, by instances of the perpetrators of such acts going unpunished, the lawless in spirit, are encouraged to become lawless in practice; and having been used to no restraint but dread of punishment, they thus become, absolutely unrestrained. Having ever regarded Government as their deadliest bane, they make a jubilee of the suspension of its operations and pray for nothing so much, as its total annihilation. While, on the other hand, good men, men who love tranquility, who desire to abide by the laws, and enjoy their benefits, who would gladly spill their blood in the defense of their country; seeing their property destroyed; their families insulted, and their lives endangered; their persons injured; and seeing nothing in prospect that forebodes a change for the better; become tired of, and disgusted with, a Government that offers them no protection; and are not much averse to a change in which they imagine they have nothing to lose. Thus, then, by the operation of this mobocratic spirit, which all must admit, is now abroad in the land, the strongest bulwark of any Government . . . may effectually be broken down and destroyed.
. . .

Let every American, every lover of liberty, every well wisher to his posterity swear by the blood of the Revolution, never to violate in the least particular, the laws of the country; and never to tolerate their violation by others. As the patriots of '76 did to the support of the Declaration of Independence, so to the support of the Constitution and Laws, let every American pledge his life, his property, and his sacred honor; let every man remember that to violate the law, is to trample on the blood of his father, and to tear the character of his own, and his children's liberty. Let reverence for the laws be breathed by every American mother to the lisping babe that prattles on her lap—let it be taught in schools, in seminaries, and in colleges; let it be written in Primers, spelling books, and in Almanacs; let it be preached from the pulpit, proclaimed in legislative halls, and enforced in courts of justice.

The speaker was Abramah Lincoln. It was his first major address, made at Springfield, Illinois, on January 27, 1838. I have no doubt whatever that Lincoln would have agreed with Judge Youngdahl that our freedom must be "freedom under God and under the law."

6

Alcohol and I

SOON AFTER I became a city commissioner I had to wrestle hard over one matter—the issuance of licenses for the sale of beer and liquor.

Alcohol is something I hate passionately, and my opposition to its use in any form is well known. The commission that governs Mobile must pass on all applications for liquor licenses, and I felt that little good would come of simply voting no every time an application was presented to the commission. For one thing, Mobile County is wet. The sale of alcohol within the county was legalized by popular vote before I came to Mobile twenty years ago, and that fact cannot be changed by wishful thinking. In my office, I have to deal with realities. There is no question that some applications for licenses should be rejected, while others merit far more consideration. Clearly, liquor licenses presented a definite challenge to my political stewardship, and I had to seek the Lord's will in prayer to know what to do.

When the commission receives a liquor application, we send a man from our licensing department to survey the nearby area. He interviews residents and owners of other business places in the area and reports back. If there are local objections for granting the new license, or if we find that the applicant has a police record, I vote no. Since two votes out of three are decisive, my own negative vote has led to the denial of a number of applications.

But what about the other cases? Sometimes a restaurant

owner believes he has to serve liquor to meet his competition, and for other reasons a man may request a license. If he has a clean record and if no one in his area objects to his plans, I simply abstain from voting. Then granting the license is up to the other two commissioners.

Some have criticized me for this policy, but I have never voted for the issuance of a liquor license, nor do I intend to. I do believe it is proper in some cases to vote neither for nor against. I received a letter from one woman, after I had tried to explain this policy, asking me how I, as a Christian, could vote in approval of some liquor licenses. In my reply I went through it all again, pointing that that I did not approve of alcohol and I do *not* vote to license its sale. I know too much about drinking for that.

My wife, Reecie, and I were married when I was seventeen, and thanks to the help of Reecie's parents, I had my own grocery store before I was eighteen. At twenty-one I was running a large wholesale business, distributing flour and feed to various groceries in Mobile and southern Alabama.

Although I greatly enjoyed my work and my contacts with my salesmen and our customers, I never felt that I had quite reached the place where I belonged. A feeling that is hard to describe, a restless sense of frustration and insecurity, haunted me day and night. I had almost anything a man could desire, but I knew that somehow something was missing—something to give meaning to my life.

Like many young people, I had started dabbling in things I should have left alone, and I took certain pride in drinking beer or whiskey with friends. It was not long before I was spending more and more time drinking, and giving less and less to my work. One of the tragedies of modern life is that so many men are as I was then—going through the motions of their work, physically on the job, but doing only a fraction of what they are capable of, because they are so groggy from too many drinks the night before.

My business was definitely on the downgrade, but my mind was often so befogged that I paid litle attention to the danger signs—the warning financial statements, the reports that showed I was not making any money, the creditors' bills that kept piling up. Each month I would coast along with the hope that things would take an upturn the next months, but that upturn never came. Then, there were accounts receivable that could not be collected, even though I kept up my wishful thinking that the money would come in.

The end came abruptly. My company was declared bankrupt.

I was fortunate in getting a job representing the H. C. Cole Milling Company of Chester, Illinois. I sold flour to the wholesalers in the Mobile area, and worked with the wholesalers' salesmen in specialty work. I would visit various stores with individual salesmen, telling the retailers how they might better promote our flour.

It was on one of these sales trips that I met a young man who did more to change my whole life than anyone else I can think of. His name was Joe Pope.

Joe was a salesman from Robertsdale, Alabama, who enjoyed drinking and carousing just as much as I did. Many were the nights we spent going from one roadhouse to another, both convinced that we were having the greatest time possible.

One day I noticed a startling change in Joe. He was happier than I had ever know him to be, but when we stopped at the restaurant where we often got sandwiches and beer for lunch he said, "I'm never going to take another drink as long as I live."

"Are you kidding?" I asked.

"Lambert," Joe said with great excitement in his voice, "I'm a Christian! Last week my friend Bill Faulk invited me to a revival meeting at First Baptist Church. You know, the one right in the middle of Robertsdale. I didn't feel much like going. But Lambert, for the first time in my life I understood what the Bible is all about, and I took Christ as my Saviour.

"All the things I've done that I'd like to forget—all my sins—are gone, Lambert! Buried in the depths of deepest sea! I wish I could tell you how happy and peaceful I am now. Sunday I took my family to church, and it was such a great feeling sitting there with them and lisening to the Word of God and singing the hymns. Why don't you let God have his will in your life?"

I mumbled an excuse. I was really worried; I was afraid Joe had lost his mind.

What he said about being a Christian didn't make much of an impression on me at the time. I had been baptized years before. Most of my friends and customers were Christian in name, and, frankly, I didn't put much stock in the way some of them lived. Neither was I very happy about the change in Joe's habits. Now he didn't tell dirty jokes, and although he still spent many evenings with me, it was usually over coffee or cokes. "Holy Joe" told me he had found what he had always searched for, and he tried to help me find it too. However, there seemed to be a veil over my eyes; his testimony meant very little to me.

One Sunday in the fall of 1956 I was surprised to get a telephone call from Joe's boss, Bob Linden, with shocking news. Joe had been driving down the highway U.S. 90

when another car crashed into his in a head-on collision. The other driver was a naval aviation cadet from Corry Field at Pensacola, Florida. The two cars telescoped into each other and swung completely around, each reversing its direction as they skidded off the road. The cadet was pinned inside his car, which was jammed together like an accordion. Joe was thrown through his windshield. Both men were killed.

I went to Joe's funeral in Robertsdale. As I stood by his casket, it came home to me that there was a better way than the way I had been living for so many years, and Joe had found that way. Although I did not realize it, God was beginning to break the bonds around my sinful heart.

But Satan was still in the saddle. Before I returned home from Joe's funeral, I was under the influence of alcohol. For a number of years I had had no interest in the things of God, and I was still far from my Saviour.

Although Reecie and I had now lived in Mobile for for ten years, and in this same community for more than five years, I had never been to church except to an occasional funeral; no one had invited us. About the only people in our neighborhood whom I knew were the tavern operators, but when God begins working, He times everything perfectly. On Thursday night after Joe's funeral, three ladies frm the Riverside Baptist Church, where my family and I are now proud to be members, knocked on our door. They were humble, friendly, kind and Christ-like. They invited Reecie and me to church, and we promised to go. That Sunday morning we were in Riverside Church.

A few weeks later I moved my church membership fom the little country church Granddaddy had helped build to Riverside Baptist Church. I was still not a Christian, but I started going to the men's class of the Riverside Sunday School, and here God began to convict me of my sins. But

I didn't want to give up any of the habits I loved, and for three months I fought God.

Now it was as though a tornado was sweeping through my soul. I had to hold hard to the things of the world, fearful that they would be swept away. At the same time, I could feel the burden of my sin growing heavier and heavier.

Four months after Joe's death, on March 2, 1957, it happened. I attended a sales demonstration in Robertsdale and tanked up afterward. On the way home, sick at heart from my sins and sick at the stomach from too much whisky, I pulled off the road and opened the door to get some fresh air.

I fell out—onto my knees.

With the gravel pressing into my kneecaps, I realized for the first time in my life exactly where I was headed. My life was going downhill, and some day I wold be lying in a casket like Joe. What then? Joe had found peace with God. What could I take into eternity but sin and shame?

If tradition or ancestry could save anyone, I would have been saved many times. My grandfather had been a deacon in the Baptist church for more than seventy years. The church I went to as a boy had been built on land donated by Granddaddy with money he had given. There I had been baptized, in his creek. If church membership could save, I had no worries, but I knew I needed something more.

Kneeling there by the side of the road, I prayed. "Lord, I'm tired of running. I'm tired of sin, tired of this life I've been living. I'm tired of all these heartaches and all this misery. Lord, I come to you know as humbly as I know how, in the name of the Lord Jesus Christ. God, have mercy on my wretched soul."

God heard that prayer. He has changed my life so completely that now it's hard to believe I'm the same man. The fact is, I'm not. "If any man be in Christ, he is a new creature: old things are passed away; . . . [and] become new" (2 Corinthians 5:17). Anything I ever accomplish will be because God reached down into the depths of sin and lifted me up and set my feet on a rock. He has put a new song in my heart and joy into my soul, and thanks to Him, I'm a new man. Reecie knew something had changed me almost as soon as she saw me. My son, Dale, knew I was a different Daddy when I stopped drinking and started praying and reading the Bible with him and Reecie. Now I *wanted* to go to church every time there was a service.

Reecie bought me a Bible and I literally wore the covers off it. I read and searched and dug and prayed; I asked the Lord to reveal his Word to me, and God blessed me in a wonderful way. I was like a desert traveler, nearly dead from starvation and thirst, who comes to a green oasis. When I got in my car, instead of turning on the radio I talked to my Lord; on trips I would spend hours meditating and praising my Saviour. And I became actively involved in every part of the church work except the women's missionary society.

That time on my knees by the side of the road was by far the greatest experience of my life, but it didn't just happen. Some time later I discovered one of the amazing links in the chain that finally brought me to God.

While visiting some sick friends at a hospital, I noticed a light-complexioned black man in the corridor who strangely attracted my attention. He wore a robe and was reading a newspaper, and I realized that he must be a patient. As our eyes met, there was a mutual feeling of recognition. My mind started racing as I walked toward him, trying to remember who this man was, and where I had known him. Suddenly he tossed his newspaper aside, jumped to his feet and called my name.

At that point I recognized this man. Fletcher English was a merchant from a small town near Mobile; he had been a customer of mine many years before. His store was the last one I visited on Monday night—the last call I made after I passed the local liquor store. While I was writing up Fletcher's order and pricing my other orders from the day's sales, I would have several drinks; many times I left Fletcher's store heavily under the influence of whisky.

How glad Fletcher and I were to see each other. After we had exchanged the usual greetings, he remarked that I looked like a new man. I said, "I *am* a new man." I told him what Christ had done in my life; how He had changed me completely.

Tears streamed down Fletcher's cheeks. "Hallelujah!" he said. "Praise God. Thank you, Jesus." His face was full of joy and I rejoiced with him, not knowing exactly what was going on but just happy because he was happy. Then I learned why Fletcher was so full of joy. He told me that for ten years he and his wife had been praying for me. Night after night they would get down on their knees and ask God to save me before it was too late. Fletcher went on to say that they had placed my name before their entire church for prayer so that God might spare my life and work a miracle in my heart.

Fletcher and his wife were concerned about me. Their church was concerned. A whole company of believers had prevailed in prayer for me. Ten years before I knew anything about it, these people had presented my name before the throne of grace. Do you wonder that I believe in God and in prevailing prayer?

7

The Next Step in
Race Relations

IT HAS SOMETIMES been said that Mobile has been lucky in race relations. It is true that there is a fine spirit between the white and the black communities of our city. We are indeed thankful that, as of the date of writing this book, we have avoided the kind of demonstrations and riots that have plagued so many American cities.

But there is no such thing as luck when it comes to people getting along with one another. It doesn't matter whether it's in a marriage or among neighbors, friends, communities, cities or states, for a harmonius relationship to exist, there must be cooperation and effort on the part of all concerned. Mobile's good record in race relations is no accident. It has taken hard work and many long hours of unselfish patience on the part of many of our citizens to create the wholesome atmosphere we have today.

I will not pretend that everything has been rosy in this area. The city commission promised the black citizens of Mobile that we would visit their neighborshoods personally and meet with the leaders of the various communities to learn what the different problems were. In one of the first communities we visited, we found a disturbing situation. In addition to the people of the neighborhood who came to the meeting, there was a large number of outsiders. Some were from other parts of the city and some were from far away. Most of these were militant blacks, but many were clergymen—Protestant ministers, Catholic priests and nuns. For nearly three hours these people accused and tried to intimidate their city fathers. Never in my life have I seen such abuse of public officials. We discontinued the neighborhood meetings.

Recently I was asked, during a television news conference, whether we were going to resume these meetings. I made the statement that I do not intend to go back to a meeting like that again, to be abused and harrassed by militant irresponsibles whose aim, as far as some of us could determine, is simply to disrupt the whole city. I do not believe that the people who elected us to the city commission would endure this kind of thing, and neither will we.

As I have mentioned, we have several militant groups in Mobile. One group is known as Neighborhood Organized Workers, or NOW. This organization planned to bring Stokely Carmichael to our twelve-million-dollar Municipal Auditorium, and the auditorium's board advised the commissioners against renting it for that purpose. Such a trail of fires and riots has followed Carmichael across the United States that our citizens overwhelmingly opposed bringing people of this type into our city. When the rental of the auditorium was refused, NOW brought Carmichael to town anyway, and he spoke at an abandoned church.

The first time Carmichael spoke there, a number of interested representatives from the FBI, the Justice Department, the state attorney general's office and other groups, were there. He spoke of things he admired about Castro and Ho Chi Minh, filling his hearers' minds with things that were not good, but he avoided saying anything for which he could be arrested.

Later on NOW held a closed meeting at which Carmichael spoke again. It has been reported that at this meeting

61

instructions were given for instituting guerrilla warfare, making Molotov cocktails, and the like. Of what he said we have no definite proof, but we do know that within two weeks of the Carmichael visit, there were a number of mysterious fires. The burning of a furniture store, an auto parts building and a mental health building created heavy losses. We have had a number of fire bombings since, and a great deal of pressure from NOW, even though it has only about two hundred members.

Of course, the majority of the blacks in Mobile, like the majority in most places, are law-abiding and peaceful. Despite its small size, NOW is very militant. The members say openly that if they can't have what they want, no one else is going to have it, even if they have to burn down the town.

When the leader of NOW made a statement of this kind at a public meeting, I notified him immediately that anyone caught disrupting anything is going to be in trouble. One of these nights our special police detail will catch someone tossing a fire bomb, and it is going to be too bad for that person.

In August, 1968, NOW wrote me a letter demanding that we create a police review board, establish what it called a truth center requiring the news media to report more news of things interesting about the black people, create a department of human relations headed by a black man, and appoint a Negro to an administrative position on the staff of the auditorium. Some of the demands were patently ridiculous. For example, all positions with our municipal government are based on civil service examinations. The names of those who pass the examinations are put on a certified list and a particular job must be filled from one of the top three names. We could no more guarantee a Negro a job than we could promise that we would hire a German, an Italian or anyone else of a particular creed or color. Race, national origin, and the like, must not and shall not enter into our hiring practices.

Some have said that we should lower our civil service standards so that more blacks can be hired. But there is no way to do this; nor would it seem right even if we could do it. When we hire someone, whether it is a secretary or an engineer, we need someone who can do the work. Anything less will not do, either in private enterprise or in the public service, but some people do not seem to realize this.

We do not believe our city needs the boards and positions demanded. Since these would waste the taxpayers money and since our hiring practices forbid the hiring of anyone simply because of race, we refused NOW's demands.

NOW then began picketing the Municipal Auditorium, succeeding for some time in keeping many people out of it. Certain social organizations and black groups who had previously used our auditorium decided not to cross the picket line and stopped renting it. We appealed to everyone to continue using the auditorium, as it is our sincere conviction that the responsible people of our community should not be kept away from one of their finest buildings by a group of militant irresponsibles whose chief aim appears to be to disrupt the peace of our municipality. We appealed especially to the responsible black majority to be willing to stand up and be counted. Here, we believe, lies the direction for continuing good race relations.

Race relations in our city have a good foundation. As far back as 1942, our municipal government saw a need for hiring Negroes. The first black man hired by the city as a classified employee was as a fireman. Today there are

63

twenty-eight Negroes in our city fire department. In 1943, the first Negro Playground and Community Center Director was employed. Today there are ten black directors and many black employees in our recreation department. The first Negro patrolman was admitted to the Mobile police department in 1954. Today there are thirty black patrolmen, one a detective, who was recently named Patrolman of the Year. In 1960, the Mobile City Lines employed their first Negro bus driver. Not long afterward, the Mobile County Sheriff's Department began to use Negro deputies. In many areas of our municipal life, Negro employment has continued to expand.

The Mobile City Commission created a special Advisory Commission in 1963. One of the first things I did after being elected a city commissioner was to attend a meeting of this special commission which has been little known to many Mobilians in spite of its quietly effective activities. I discovered that the commission, which consists of eight white and four black members, meets twice a month and provides the city commission with a readily accessible group of informed citizens to whom it may turn for advice, information, and recommendations in many areas of public concern. It also provides communication between the various interests concerned with broad community problems. It was created to give special attention to such matters as human relations, and moral and social problems. Operating without fanfare or publicity, the Special Advisory Commission has solved many urban problems.

This commission has the confidence of Mobile's Negro community; therefore, it has been able to cool off the Rap Browns and the Stokely Carmichaels who might otherwise have fanned flames of hate. When Martin Luther King and others wanted to come into Mobile for rallies, demonstrations and boycotts, the black community refused to cooperate, largely because of the efforts of the Special Advisory Commission. It was this group that prevented a demonstration before the national television cameras during a Junior Miss Pageant in the Municipal Auditorium, also preventing a sympathy march during the unfortunate incidents in Selma.

If any of this sounds in any way negative, let me point out that the Special Advisory Commission has been able to persuade various business leaders in our city of the reasonableness of many Negro requests for service on an equal basis with whites. Meetings with these leaders led to the opening of lunch counters for non-segregated service long before many other Southern cities—and many Northern places of business—had taken this step. The commission has been fortunate in obtaining employment for qualified Negroes in banks, department stores, utility offices, and many other places where there were color barriers only a few years ago. This project of finding jobs for qualified Negroes, and finding Negroes for available jobs, is being financed by local businessmen.

The Special Advisory Commission set up an office for handling employment and created the position of Job Coordinator, capably held by the Reverend Charles Tunstall, a Negro minister. He has been instrumental in placing a number of Negroes in jobs, and his efforts have been well received by white business leaders. As Mr. Tunstall puts it, "When they find out that I'm not a blackjack man, and that my job is to build a better community through harmonious race relations, they are put at ease." Needless to say, no pressure is used against any employer by Mr. Tunstall; he simply tries to place trustworthy and qualified Negroes in various levels of our economic society. Those

Negroes who know they must produce to get ahead in this world are the ones we are able to help through our Job Coordinator's Office.

In addition, the Mobile Area Committee for Training and Development is doing a wonderful job providing blacks with skills such as welding and shipfitting. Our local trade school has helped greatly in the advance of the Negro race in our community.

In the summer of 1968, the city commission initiated a program of hiring underprivileged young people. We set up centers in six areas of Mobile where these teen-agers could apply for jobs. We considered only applications from those whose family income was less than $3000. Most of the six hundred young people we hired were Negroes. They were employed for six weeks of the summer in our public works, traffic engineering, parks and electrical departments. This was the first time some of these young people had ever held jobs. We gave them an opportunity to work, and showed them that they could make some money through skill and effort. Some of them learned to work for the first time in their lives, and all of them accomplished a great deal. The program worked beautifully and we are very pleased with what happened. Now those six hundred young people are back in high school and college, and their studies mean more to them because they have tasted the meaning and the fruits of worthwhile employment.

Today Mobile is without a doubt the South's most integrated city, and this has been brought about with very little trouble or confusion. The single exception to date is the dastardly bombing of the home of a civil rights worker.

In the area of Negro race relations and employment in our area, we can see many accomplishments during the past twenty years, especially in the last ten. When one looks at a city like Birmingham, with not one Negro policeman, one wonders if that city could not have avoided much trouble if it had had the foresight of Mobile. Important positions held by Negroes here, in addition to those already mentioned, include those of electrician, building inspector, clerk, secretary, concessions attendant, ticket seller, school traffic officer, truck driver, and heavy equipment operator.

Mobile county schools were desegregated in 1963. At present more than twelve hundred Negro students attend bi-racial schools in the county. The high school with the largest number of black students is the Ben C. Rain High School, where my seventeen-year-old son, Dale, is a junior. I am happy to report also, that all four of Mobile's institutions of higher learning have Negro students.

If we are to continue to make progress in race relations, we must have reasonable citizens, both black and white. We who are white must face the facts and admit that the Negro has been oppressed in many areas. We must confess that during the past century Negroes have been discriminated against in many ways. We must recognize that we live in a new era; that yesterday is past, and all people, regardless of race, color or creed, are entitled to equal rights. Reasonable white men must no longer deny any man an opportunity for advancement because of his color; and reasonable white men must allow all qualified men to advance as doors of opportunity open.

We can no longer live in the days of our forefathers. Negroes no longer live down the lane and pick cotton. The black man has been thrust into society. It matters not whether we like this fact. There is no escape! This problem must be faced.

As reasonable men accept the challenges before them,

these problems can be worked out. There are some who feel guilty, evidently, of their forefathers' sins. Reasonable men must forget the past. What my grandfather did, or what my great-grandfather did, I cannot help. Here I am today, living in a modern society with many complex problems. I must try to live in peace with my fellow man, whoever he may be.

Reasonable white men must also realize the predicament of the blacks. Since the 1954 civil rights decision, the American Negro has made much progress, and many white men have changed their attitudes toward the race issue. However, many thousands of Negroes find themselves totally unprepared to assume their places of responsibility in society.

Reasonable white men must realize that the Negro needs training and education, and that in many cases he needs to be advanced culturally. Reasonable white men must patiently go through this period of adjustment. We must provide opportunities for the Negro to become qualified, and once he is qualified, provide an opportunity for him to prove himself.

For our country to be the prosperous, progressive nation we want it to be, every citizen, regardless of color, must be productive. This is the goal that is before us. Every unproductive citizen is a burden on those who are productive. To have every American working must be our goal.

Negroes also must be reasonable. They will have to realize that the events of a hundred years cannot be changed in the snap of a finger. The militant Negroes want everything now. This is impossible. The businessman starts small and grows. The farmer plants seed and cultivates before he gets a harvest. It is my firm conviction that the shouts and demands of the Negro that the position of the

Negro race as a whole be changed *now*, will never get the job done. If those who shout, "Now!" would spend half their energy trying to help the Negro advance, they would accomplish far more.

Every person, regardless of race, must want to advance himself as an individual. He must have initiative. He must want to get ahead, financially, educationally and culturally. I am where I am today because I determined that I didn't want to spend my life in a cotton patch. I made up my mind to do something about it. It has not come easily. Had I not worked hard, I would still be in the cotton patch.

The reasonable Negro must realize that the members of his race must work hard and that they must put out a great deal of effort to be successful in a free enterprise system. It is impossible—*absolutely impossible*—to get something for nothing.

During the Poor People's March on Washington, a man from Mississippi said to Secretary of Agriculture, Orville Freeman, "We aren't begging for nothing that don't belong to us. We want it, and we want it now." This is certainly not reason. Just because John Doe has plenty, and has worked hard to get it, is no sign for him to give it to me when I haven't done anything to earn it. For me to take the attitude that a part of his goods is mine, is ridiculous.

For 150 marchers to walk into a cafeteria in the Department of Agriculture (which incidentally does not belong to the government but to private enterprise), and eat $292.00 worth of food, and then say that the Negro is owed this and refuse to pay the bill, is far from the realm of the reasonable.

For Ralph Abernathy to say on television, "I've come to Washington to raise hell," and, "We will turn this place upside down," is beyond reason.

For Miss Miriam Wright, a Negro lawyer representing the Poor People's March, to say,"We are asking you to respond or we will have to lash out. We will have to fight with guns or fire," is still further beyond reason.

For a dozen Negroes to walk into a Pensacola, Florida, shoe store, take shoes from the shelves and walk out without paying, or for Rap Brown or Stokely Carmichael to say, "If a whitie gets in your way, kill him," is certainly far from reasonable.

If the Negro is to advance, he must stop this nonsense.I can deal with a reasonable person, and I will face any problem that comes up in a sensible way; but I will not make decisions because of threats, nor will I tolerate in our city some of the things that are going on in other parts of our country.

Still, I believe Mobile has a bright future in race relations. With the programs I have noted, with more emphasis on Negro education, with more understanding on the part of the white community of the problems of our age, and with the active interest of our city officials, I am certain that we will continue to forge ahead.

There are a number of things we must do. We must continue to improve our neighborhoods through code enforcement. We must continue the fight to eliminate poverty by giving peoples of all races an opportunity to advance. We must be concerned about the health and welfare of our neighbors. We must keep on providing playgrounds and recreational programs for our young people. We must create such an atmosphere of progressiveness and togetherness that when the Rap Browns and Stokely Carmichaels come along, our people will tell them, "Don't stop here, for we have a good thing going—a city of all the

70

people, where the war on poverty is working because everyone has an opportunity to work."

The future of race relations depends on each one of us. Every citizen, especially the business and the civic leader, must put his hand to the plow and break new ground in a way that will make those who follow proud of what we accomplished.

8

The Crisis of the Cities

IF THERE IS anything I have learned in the past few years, it is that this country has an urban crisis, and that almost every municipality and urban area is plagued with many challenges of broad social and economic consequence. Problems of employment, education, housing, urban renewal, pollution, traffic, sanitation, recreation, assistance for the underprivileged and adequate fire and police protection confront every city official in the United States.

I have also learned that government alone cannot solve the many complex problems of the urban crisis. I am firmly convinced that the challenge of the cities calls for greater commitment on the part of business. Effective, long-range solutions to our many urban problems hinge on greater cooperation between business and government.

Such cooperation has been attempted with a great deal of success on the national level by the formation of the Urban Coalition. Top executives from the country's largest industries and businesses have worked with the national administration to make great strides in many areas, especially in on-the-job training. Ford, Chrysler, and many other companies have begun helping the untrained become trained and productive. Although there was no great optimism that a high proportion of these people would remain long on their new jobs, the Ford Motor Company found that the retention rate of those hired was seventy-eight percent, and other businesses had similar success. Much

72

more cooperation of this kind between business and government is needed. Urban affairs are primarily the responsibility of business. When a city grows, so does business; when it fails to prosper, business will not prosper. If a city needs additional roads and expressways to get people to the business district, it stands to reason that business should be the most interested. If there are riots and strife, business is the first to suffer, and I do not see how businessmen can divorce their interests from such crises.

Businessmen have contributed much to the progress of my own city of Mobile. Some of their finest representatives serve on our boards and commissions and give the city government the benefit of their knowledge. The Chamber of Commerce, the Jaycees, and many other service clubs and organizations are ready and willing to help whenever they are called upon. However, I am afraid that the average businessman feels that he has discharged his civic responsibilities when he has paid his taxes and has gone to the polls to vote. He elects the city commission and then says, "Okay, men, it's up to you. Run our town. Provide us with safety, sanitation, good streets and all the other things that go with your job. It's all yours!"

Let me say that responsible officials can handle the administration of government, but there is a vast difference between routine municipal operations and the challenges that face the cities today. Government alone cannot do the job. During the past few decades, our cities have gone through a tremendous change. The population of our country, once largely rural, is now overwhelmingly urban. Seventy percent of all Americans live in the cities, and occupy only two percent of the land area. The great influx of urban centers has caused a terrific increase in metropolitan business, but it has also caused many problems.

The urban areas have expanded greatly. As homes are built farther and farther away from the inner city, services such as water, sewers, paved streets, lighting and police protection are demanded and expected. At the same time, the central core of each city begins to deteriorate. Whole sections of American cities, which were fine residential and business areas twenty-five years ago are now slums, in desperate need of rebuilding. Then, as the people move outward, business also moves, causing blighted business districts. In our growing affluence, there are more and more automobiles; many families have two or more, and these are all on the streets at one time. Antiquated two-lane streets can no longer handle the increased burden placed upon them. In turn, the number of individuals using public transportation has been reduced, causing a reduction in service and producing greater hardships for those dependent on buses and subways.

Along with the influx of urban areas, of course, there is the population explosion and the problem of automation. Today, there is far more competition in the labor market and a growing need for people to become trained and qualified for certain jobs. Literally millions of workers are totally unprepared for the future, and these people must be helped. In addition, the average life span has been lengthened by modern medicine. Nine percent of America's population is over sixty-five, and there is a much greater need for homes for the aged. Add to all this the need for parks and playgrounds, for pollution control, for beautification programs, for more adequate police protection, and the need for additional revenues, along with the many social and racial problems of the cities, and I think you will realize why I say that government cannot do the job alone. It is imperative for government to enlist the know-how, the resources and the brain power of private business to meet these needs. Businessmen had more justification for ignoring problems like these a few years ago, but that time is past. Now business must look beyond its own limited interests and become involved in the crisis of the cities.

The first step is overcoming the communication gap between business and government. No doubt one reason business has not become more involved is its lack of awareness of the problems. Few people really understand the operations of their local government. I must confess that before I ran for municipal office , I myself knew very little about the workings of the government of Mobile. While there are hundreds of businessmen in this city, I doubt whether one percent has ever been inside City Hall, much less attended a weekly meeting of the city commission. To bridge this communication gap, we have made a special effort to invite the businessmen of the community to visit City Hall and attend our weekly commission meeting. I believe that government must admit its failure to communicate its problems to the business community, and then translate urban problems to those in management, cultivate their support, and generate the enthusiasm that will insure their help.

Many urban problems are environmental, relating to housing, job training, basic education, race relations, health problems, and the like. Let's think first about housing. Many slums are being reclaimed through urban renewal programs which depend on federal funds for two-thirds of their support. Many such areas are so deteriorated that I do not believe there is any other way to rebuild them. It is almost certain that public housing is here to stay, and it has been encouraged by the lack of interest in low-income housing on the part of private enterprise. But in the renewal areas, there is much land available for private business to build housing for the under-privileged. I am thoroughly convinced that free enterprise can build apartment complexes which are durable, attractive, and within the reach of the family with low income. In some cities this is already being done; various businesses have united and formed associations to buy run-down property and rehabilitate it for the poor. Some firms have carried out their own housing rehabilitation. Smith, Kline & French rebuilt more than a hundred homes in a deteriorating Philadelphia neighborhood. Similar rejuvenation has been done by the United States Gypsum Company in Harlem, by Eastern Gas & Fuel in Boston, and by Eli Lilly & Company in Indianapolis.

Then, let's look at the area of job training. Some businesses and industries are making a fine contribution to this by instituting excellent job training programs. The First National Bank in New York, the Caterpillar Tractor Company of East Peoria, Illinois, and the J. L. Hudson Company of Detroit are training and hiring people who previously had been considered unemployable. Television stations and labor unions have helped a great many such individuals find jobs. The National Alliance of Businessmen has set the goal of hiring and training 500,000 hard-core unemployed by 1971. Its first year's quota of 100,000 already has been more than met.

However, among this nation's millions of businessmen there are many who have taken no positive action toward reducing the number of unemployed in the inner cities. Merchants, for example, who need clerks, cashiers and other workers tell me that if they could just get qualified help, they would hire them. Let's look at this matter. Merchants need qualified help; unqualified people need jobs.

Why not get the two together? Perhaps one merchant alone could not conduct a program like the one I have in mind, but in that case a number of merchants could unite their efforts. I believe these businessmen could conduct schools for from six to eight weeks, using their own experienced managerial personnel as instructors to train prospective employees. I have challenged the businessmen of Mobile to find employees in this way from among persons who would otherwise never be qualified for a good job, and to do more on-the-job training. I believe every businessman in the nation should ask himself what he can do in this direction. For as long as a man is not productive, when he could become so, he is a burden to the rest of us. Every American who can, must learn to produce; business must give him that opportunity. The goal of every one of us should be to have every American working.

There is a need for business to conduct special summer youth programs. We must get idle teen-agers off the streets and into jobs where they can learn the pleasure of accomplishment and its rewards. Our youth must realize that no one gets something for nothing, and that to share in the benefits of the free enterprise system each person must apply himself.

Business should also take a more active part in programs to encourage young people to stay in school. Every year thousands of them drop out. One thing many businesses throughout this country are doing is providing personnel to speak to high-school groups, assuring them that jobs await those who continue their education and pointing out the need for a good basic training in our increasingly complex, scientific society. More of this should be done, and all of us might well take another look at our local school systems from the viewpoint of how they are preparing our youth for today's problems, and how they can be strengthened.

There also must be a greater involvement of business in community relations. Although Mobile has made great strides in this area, with many merchants contributing funds for a special job-coordinator office, many have taken the attitude, "Let City Hall do it." Again I say that government cannot do this job alone. I call on business to meet this challenge of community relations. The first way to meet it is to give all persons, regardless of race, opportunities for employment. Early in 1969 the F. W. Woolworth Company signed a one-million-dollar contract with a black construction company to build a new store with 55,000 square feet of floor space in Harlem. It is anticipated that the employees will be residents of Harlem. After the riots in Watts, the Aerojet-General Corporation founded a company there which employs five hundred local workers. As this is being written, the Avco Corporation is constructing a new printing plant in Boston which will train and use members of minority groups. If America is to have a future worthy of its ideals, more efforts must be made by firms of all sizes to improve the housing and the work opportunities of the underprivileged communities in our cities.

There is also an urgent need for business to get behind clean-up and beautification programs. Here again the local governing bodies need industrial support. I believe each firm could start well within its own walls. If each business began a program against litter and mess, more employees would be made aware of the high cost of litter removal and the fact that tax dollars spent for this purpose could be used for more worthwhile projects.

Another whole category of urban problems could be called business-oriented, the problems that directly affect business, such as transportation, parking, streets, express-ways, crime and taxation. While I will not attempt to elaborate on all these problems, I would like to emphasize the lack of funds to do the things that need to be done.

There is noone who is not concerned about adequate police protection, adequate fire protection, adequate means of transportation, adequate streets and roads, adequate sanitation, adequate public works and public service. All these require adequate revenue. The policemen of Mobile are doing a good job, but we need to beef up the force with more men, better equipment and more adequate pay. As a commissioner, and as the mayor of my city, I have fought for pay increases for all city employees, and now we need further increases to keep our employees and attract others. Our local system of public transportation must be maintained, and it may be that the only way to do this will be to have the city take over the system. In Mobile and in all the cities I know, additional sources of revenue must be found, and business must help meet this challenge. The business community can unite its efforts, its know-how and brainpower, to study new ways of meeting the fiscal problems of the city. When it comes up with recommendations, it can use its influence to educate the public as to what must be done. Business also can influence legislators to help equalize taxes on a state-wide basis, so that tax dollars go where the people are.

The days of the country farm are now largely behind us. The days of the company store, when a corporation owned the homes, the stores, and nearly everything else in a profitable mining community, are gone. The days of the public handout, when the majority looked to big government to solve their problems, are also receding into the past. What is needed now is the dynamic cooperation of both business and government in facing the crisis of the cities. In each municipality I believe business should move out in a united effort, perhaps through the Chamber of Commerce or some type of urban council or committee, to advise, assist and even in many cases to assume the responsibility, to meet our urban challenges. When all of us, whether in business, government or our private capacities, work together, we can again look with pride on the cities of America.

9

The Ingredients of Success

OF EVERY ONE HUNDRED men who are now twenty-five years old, statistics indicate that forty years from now one will be wealthy, four will be comfortably situated, five will be self-supporting, fifty-four will be dependent on others, and thirty-six will have died. More than half these men will be poor, facing a future in the care of their families or the government. Only ten percent will be financially successful.

Financial independence is not the only kind of success, of course, although few people would probably prefer to spend the last years of their lives as dependents. Political activity accomplishes nothing in the life of a community or nation unless it is in some way successful. An athlete is hardly admired if he never wins, and in the spiritual life, I cannot believe that God wants failures. The great Apostle Paul asked, "Know ye not that they which run in a race run all, but one receiveth the prize?" (I Corinthians 9:24).

I am confident that no matter who you are or what your circumstances may be, you can be successful. Just as it takes flour and sugar, eggs and shortening, know-how and a hot oven to make a cake, success requires certain ingredients. Although I do not pose as an authority on this subject, from my own personal observation and experience I have discovered some of the most essential of these ingredients. I am going to list them here in the hope that they will be helpful.

One important ingredients is *direction*. Many people fail because they never really set any goals in life, and never think about where they are going. They just drift until something they think is better comes along. Here is a man working in a service station. He's here today and gone tomorrow, always looking for greener pastures, while actually he is standing in acres of diamonds, for he is already in one of America's fastest growing industries. He would have all kinds of opportunities for advancement, if only he had a goal and began working toward it.

For success in anything, you must know where you are going. A few years ago a very good friend of mine went to work for a bank for less money than he could have made in a different field. My friend, however, had direction. His goal was to make a success in the world of banking. This he is doing. In twelve years he has advanced to the position of vice president. He has remained with the same institution while others have left or remained at the same desks. My friend studied, worked and achieved, because he set a goal and did everything in his power to reach it.

Whatever I have accomplished in my own life has not resulted from drifting aimlessly. From my early years I felt that I wanted to be in business for myself. Others might daydream of winning a sweepstakes or falling into an easy job. For myself, I knew that I would never be content until I had become my own boss. (Let me add that I know that many people dream of being self-employed. This is not always practical; many people can do better working for someone else.) The goal of becoming self-employed was an obsession with me.

My first business experience came before I finished high school, in the retail grocery business. I operated a commissary near my father-in-law's saw mill. When the saw mill closed, my wife and I decided to move to Mobile. There I worked in a milling company until I had the opportunity to enter the wholesale business.

After several years of operating my own feed and grocery business, as you know from earlier in this book, I lost a fortune and was flat broke. Again I went to work for someone else, becoming a manufacturer's representative for a milling concern. After four years of this, I resolved to enter the food brokerage business. This I did, starting from scratch. This business would not exist today without my early dreams and my decision to become a successful food broker.

Another ingredient vital to success is *determination*. After a person decides where he is going and sets a goal, he must take the attitude that nothing is going to prevent his reaching that goal. Whether your goal is to become the top producer in your company, or to become sales manager or president, or to build a larger business, or to succeed in some other way, to be successful you must feel that absolutely nothing can stop you.

When I entered the brokerage business I was determined to make it successful. There were many disappointments, and many dark hours. Beginning a new business was like carving a statue from stone, a chip at a time, or building a city in the wilderness, cutting one tree at a time. In spite of the slow progress I was determined to go ahead.

When I entered the race for city commissioner I was confident that this was the thing I ought to do, and from the day that I decided to run, I was determined to win.

The trouble with most of us is that we just haven't made up our minds to be successful. Napoleon Bonaparte once said, "No one but myself can be blamed for my fall." Whether he was right or wrong about that, it is certainly true that no one else is responsible for our final failure or success. We must have determination if we are to accomplish our goals.

Someone has expressed what I am saying in verse:

THINKING

If you think you are beaten, you are.
If you think you dare not, you don't.
If you like to win but think you can't.
It's almost a cinch you won't.
If you think you'll lose, you've lost.
For out in the world we find
Success begins with a fellow's will,
It's all in the state of mind.
If you think you are outclassed, you are.
You've got to think high to rise,
You've got to be sure of yourself before
You can ever win a prize.
Life's battle doesn't always go
To the stronger or faster man;
But sooner or later the man who wins
Is the man who thinks he can.

Walter D. Wintle

A third ingredient of success is *diligence.* This, of course, is closely related to determination; however, a person may have a degree of determination and still not work hard enough to accomplish his objective. One of the most important aspects of diligence is mental. We must think; we must keep our minds constantly alert to take advantage of every opportunity. Percy H. Whitney, managing director of the Dale Carnegie Courses and author of the book *Five*

Great Rules of Selling, said, "Not one salesman in ten million uses his brain as much as he could—some don't seem to use it at all—for the purpose of thinking."

A salesman once suffered a stroke but seemed to improve after the crisis was over. A friend called to ask him how he was feeling. "Fair to middling," the salesman confided. "No pain, eating and sleeping right well, and I'm able to drive, fetch the groceries and go to church." Then as an afterthought he added, "Of course my mind is gone, but I don't miss it." To be a success, a person must not be like this salesman. He must use his mind constantly. Henry L. Doherty, who was successful both in utilities and in the oil business, commended "old-fashioned brain sweat." We should use our brains more than our backs.

Diligence also calls for the exertion of every effort—not just what is expected, but a little extra.

Many persons have climbed the ladder of success by making full use of a certain force. Those who exercise this force usually outshine other people in every field of business and industry.

It is a force that can be a springboard to success for even the humblest worker: *hard work!*

If the average man fully realized what a little extra effort might do for him, it would open a new and brighter future for many who are now in a rut. The persistent exercise of a little extra effort is one of the most powerful forces contributing to success.

For it keeps a man on his toes, jogs his mind and energies, taps his inborn abilities, gives him pride and confidence, and makes it easy to bring out the best that is in him.

Author Unknown

The only real luck is hard work. To those who give their best efforts, doors of opportunity are bound to open. Do you remember the presidential election when all the polls and prophets predicted that Thomas E. Dewey would beat Harry S. Truman? President Truman's victory did not come easily; it resulted from unusual diligence and effort. Truman decided that the polls need not have the last word. He chartered a special train, traveled 31,000 miles, made 356 speeches, shook hands with 500,000 people, and talked to perhaps twenty million voters in personal appearances and to millions more by radio. He won the election, but it took hard work. The Kansas City Advertising and Sales Executives Club gave him a free lifetime membership as "The World's Greatest Salesman."

The most important ingredient of all in achieving success is *devotion*. "Man shall not live by bread alone" (Matthew 4:4). Each year we are given 8,760 hours. These hours cannot be used entirely for ourselves; we must remember the One who has granted them to us.

All my adult life I have been in business. For several years I barely got by. Although I had a wonderful opportunity to succeed when I was set up in business while still in my teens, I flopped miserably and lost everything before I was twenty-five years old. My first step toward genuine success was when I realized that it was God who had given me life, health, and 8,760 hours of time every year, and that it was to Him that I owed my supreme loyalty. The Old Testament states that it is the Lord who ". . . giveth thee power to get wealth" (Deuteronomy 8:18). Jesus said, "But seek ye first the kingdom of God, and his righteousness; and all these things shall be added unto you" (Matthew 6:33). This I believe and I find it to be true in my own life.

Many men have found, as I have, that the basic ingredient for success is devotion. R. G. Le Tourneau, Maxey

Jarman, Herbert Taylor, Henderson Belk, and many other great businessmen have found this true. J. C. Penney, founder of the famous corporation that bears his name, once said, "When a man gets so busy that he doesn't have time for God, he has more business than God intended for him to have."

James Cash Penney, who is now in his nineties, was born in Missouri to a poverty-stricken Baptist preacher. He opened his first store in Kemmerer, Wyoming, a mining village with a population of less than a thousand. His gross income for the first fiscal year was only $29,000. Today there are seventeen hundred J. C. Penney stores, grossing over three billion dollars per year, with a hundred thousand employees.

At one time, J. C. Penney lost his health plus a forty-million-dollar fortune. In 1931, confined to a sanatorium, he was depressed because he thought he was a total failure; he wrote farewell letters to his friends and family. Then he heard singing, and he made out these words:

Be not dismayed whate'er betide,
God will take care of you;
Beneath His wings of love abide,
God will take care of you.
Through every day, o'er all the way,
God will take care of you.

All you may need He will provide . . .
Nothing you ask will be denied. . . .
No matter what may be your test . . .
Lean, weary one, upon His breast,
God will take care of you.

C. D. Martin

He followed the singing to the sanatorium chapel, and

87

soon afterward he gave his life completely to God. From that day to this, he has faithfully served God with his time, talent and money.

Mr. Penney gets plenty of sleep and rest; if he does not feel well he simply takes a little time off to recuperate. Too often, many of us push ourselves until we are exhausted and we have become candidates for heart attacks. No one can expect to live out his years, or even to think clearly, if he is continually exhausted. Mr. Penney also eats well, but sparingly. I myself must be the first to admit that I do everything *but* eat sparingly! I love to eat, but I am afraid it is true that most Americans dig their graves with their teeth. In addition, Mr. Penney has disciplined himself in his personal habits; he does not indulge in tobacco or alcohol in any form. Science is just beginning to uncover the harm these narcotics do to our minds, bodies, and our very lives. Attention like this to *physical fitness* is important for success.

Let me mention another factor that has been very important in Mr. Penney's life and is imperative for anyone who wants to be truly successful: *honesty.* Some men have gained fame and fortune for a season through dishonesty, but in most cases such prosperity is brief; the sins of these men find them out sooner or later and they often end their lives destitute and abhorred. By honesty, however, I don't mean simply keeping your fingers out of the other man's till. True honesty means giving what you are paid for, giving your best to God and your fellow man. When J. C. Penney opened his first store, he was told it would be impossible to do a cash business since the town had twenty-one saloons and a number of company stores which were glad to do business on credit. Penney, however, decided that his primary responsibility was to be fair to his customers. "A customer-relationship built on credit," he has written in his autobiography, *View From the Tenth Decade*, "didn't seem to me fair either to customers or the merchant. A certain number of folks, at least would buy—or be tempted to—more than they could wisely afford if they didn't have to pay for it right off." He stuck to this principle, and his original Golden Rule Store grew into one of America's great chainstore enterprises, built on the rule set forth by Jesus Christ. Late in 1968, Mr. Penney told a reporter, "This company's success is due to the application of the Golden Rule to every individual, the public, and all of our activities." Asked if he had any advice for the ambitious, he replied: "Observe the Golden Rule and never stop learning. Always keep preparing yourself for the future."

I am afraid that far too many Americans follow the rule, "Do the other fellow before he does you." But in the greatest discourse ever uttered, the Sermon on the Mount, Christ said, "Therefore all things whatsoever ye would that men should do to you, do ye even so to them" (Matthew 7:12). In other words, "Do unto others as you would have them do unto you."

This applies in so many ways. When we criticize, I wonder how many people think of how it would feel if they were criticized. When we scold or mock, do we think of what it would be like to be scolded or mocked ourselves? I am sure that if we turned the situation around, we would be far less prone to inflict unkind thoughts and attitudes or unjust practices on others.

One thing more is *confidence* in people. J. C. Penney has trusted others throughout his career; he insists that Penney employees be known as associates, and be compensated according to their productivity. Recently, an Ohio man wrote three firms about his overdue bills, explaining that a death in the family had produced an unexpectedly high funeral bill and requesting an extension of credit. Later he wrote the Penney Company, "Yours was the only human reaction to this note. It's refreshing in this day and time to find that a company the size of Penney's still has a heart." Mr. Penney has stamped his firm with his own philosophy of confidence in his belief that people are always more important than things.

Before I became a Christian, I thought everyone was like myself. I had very little confidence in men; I am afraid I did not really trust anyone. Today I know how genuine many people are, and I have learned to trust my fellow men. This is a wonderful thing to experience. It is not true, as some would have us believe, that everyone has gone to the dogs. There are millions of good, reliable, conscientious persons in this world, and until a man proves untrustworthy, we should have confidence in him.

These are the things that contribute more than anything else, in my opinion, to success. I know that they work, and if you put them into practice in your life, they will work for you.

10

The Source of Our Liberty

A WELL-KNOWN dictionary defines liberty as freedom or release from slavery; or the sum of rights and exemptions possessed in common by the people of a community, state or nation.

American liberty, one of the most priceless portions of our heritage, is based, to a great extent, on the Declaration of Independence. If I were to suggest doing away with the Declaration, I would receive telegrams of violent protest; probably I would soon be tarred, feathered, and stoned. Yet if I were to ask you what the Declaration of Independence says, perhaps you would be embarrassed. I fear that few Americans have read its mighty words and that to millions it is a dead letter. Although it contains only 1,321 words, many do not know its truths and never take the time to discover them.

The task of drafting this great document fell to Thomas Jefferson (who was only thirty-three at the time), John Adams, Benjamin Franklin, Robert Livingston and Roger Sherman. These men made it unmistakably clear that the very foundation of freedom is God. The draft they presented to the Continental Congress contained two very deliberate references to Him.

They referred to "the laws of Nature and of Nature's God." They saw that our basic rights are rooted in universal laws which come ultimately from the creator. They added, "We hold these truths to be self-evident, that all men are created equal, that they are endowed by their Creator with certain unalienable Rights, that among these are Life, Liberty and the pursuit of Happiness." Our founding fathers confessed that man's rights stem from the gifts of God.

When the members of Congress received this first draft of the Declaration, they were not completely satisfied with it. They took it upon themselves to add two more references to God, thereby going on record before the world that they justified their action in forming a new nation by divine authority. The Declaration of Independence now reads: "We, therefore, the Representatives of the United States of America, in General Congress, Assembled, appealing to the Supreme Judge of the world for the rectitude of our intentions . . . ."Witnessing that God is the universal judge, these men appealed to Him to certify the rightness of their plans. We need men today who are not ashamed to appeal to the supreme judge for leadership, wisdom and guidance.

In the closing sentence of the independence document, Congress made a final statement of its trust in God. Consider these heart-stirring words: "And for the support of this Declaration, with a firm reliance on the protection of Divine Providence, We mutually pledge to each other our Lives, our Fortunes, and our sacred Honor." The members of the Continental Congress covenanted together in the presence of God as they launched the new ship of state. They knew that He providentially rules in the affairs of men, and they testified to their trust in His protection.

All Christians should be familiar with these references to God in our Declaration of Independence. Without this document which so strongly affirms the divine origin of our liberty and our nation, the Constitution and Bill of Rights lack a clear, solid foundation.

This liberty is not cheap. Freedom always costs something. Freedom from ignorance, for instance, costs hours of study and training. Freedom from poverty costs hard work and application of talents to definite tasks. Our freedom from the curse of sin cost God His only begotten Son. Our American freedom cost our forefathers and it cost the men who signed the Declaration of Independence.

There were fifty-six of them in all, representatives from the thirteen original states. Twenty-six signers of the Declaration were lawyers, nine were merchants, six were farmers, six were physicians; there were statesmen, soldiers, surveyors and one minister. These men suffered for you and me. Not only were they concerned with the three million inhabitants of the thirteen colonies; they were thinking of those who were to come, and they had a burning desire to secure the God-given freedoms of generations yet unborn.

John Adams of Massachusetts wrote his wife the night before he signed the Declaration of Independence: "I am well aware of the toil and blood and treasure it will cost us to maintain this Declaration." William Ellery of Rhode Island watched thoughtfully as every representative carefully affixed his signature to the famous document. "I was determined," he said, "to see how they all looked as they signed what might be their death warrant."

The Declaration was a death warrant to many. At the age of sixty-five, John Hart of New Jersey was driven from the bedside of his dying wife, his thirteen children were scattered, his four-hundred-acre farm was destroyed by fire and he was forced to live as a fugitive for a year and a half. Thomas McKean of Delaware was "hunted like a fox and disliked by those who ought to have been his friends." Five different times he had to move his family away from people who despised him so much that he feared for the lives of his wife and children.

Abraham Clark of New Jersey had two sons in the army who were taken prisoner. One nearly died of starvation when he was placed in solitary confinement because of his father's courageous action. Francis Lewis of New York had his home ransacked and burned. Far worse, his wife was taken prisoner and locked in a squalid jail, without even a change of clothing for a long period. As a result of harsh treatment, her health broke down and within two years she died. Lewis Morris of New York realized that by the stroke of his pen he was inviting disaster. He owned a luxurious manor in northern Manhattan, a thousand acres of woodland and prize herds of cattle. When he became one of the fifty-six signers it all went on the block. For six long years Morris and his family lived in poverty.

William Whipple of New Hampshire had his leg shattered by a cannon ball at the Battle of Rhode Island. A few months later, with a wooden leg, he was back serving his country in Congress. Carter Braxton of Virginia, his ships driven from the seas and his wealth wiped out by war-time inflation, lived to see his home mortgaged and his personal property, including furniture, confiscated to pay his debts.

Richard Stockton of New Jersey sacrificed his post as chief justice of the state Supreme Court by becoming a signer. He was betrayed, dragged from his bed and thrown into prison by the enemy. His private library, one of the finest in the land, was burned. His thoroughbred horses were stolen and his farm laid waste. He died prematurely, at fifty-one, broken in health by his mistreatment in prison.

Lyman Hall and George Walton of Georgia suffered, respectively, confiscation of property and imprisonment. Joseph Hewes and William Hooper of North Carolina also paid a heavy price. Hewes died from overwork. Hooper and his family were driven from their home. Thomas Heyward, Arthur Middleton and Edward Rutledge of South Carolina, following their signing the Declaration, were taken prisoner in battle. They suffered privations and indignities for ten harsh months.

Yes, liberty always costs. Do we really appreciate it? Let us avoid the widespread unconcern and lack of appreciation for the freedom we enjoy.

What can we do personally to see that our liberty is preserved? We ought to take time to read the Declaration of Independence. Yes, it is hard to read. It is very technical and difficult, but so are other papers that we read. Remember, next to the Bible, these are 1,321 of the most important words on earth. Let us familiarize ourselves with them.

Then, we can tell others about the Declaration. If we had a new car, a new home, or a new business venture, we would want to tell people. Let's tell them about this good news, our liberty. Acquaint them with the basic highlights of the Declaration of Independence and encourage one and all to read it.

Third, we should see that the Declaration is taught in the classroom. It must be taught; our children must be brought up to appreciate it.

We must do more than repeat that all men are endowed by their Creator with certain unalienable rights. We must take positive steps to insure that political, religious, economic, educational, social, racial, legal and cultural rights of all persons without exception are respected, protected and fulfilled.

We must stand up and be counted for our rights and we must stand for our fellow man who may not be as well versed and informed. We must have courage for our own good and for the good of our neighbor who may not have enough courage. We must be willing to suffer—to suffer persecution, if need be, as our forefathers did for the liberty that we enjoy today.

May God help us to understand, prize and protect our priceless liberty. May our land forever be the land of the free and the home of the brave.

11

When God Gets One Hundred Percent

FROM THE MOMENT I gave myself to Christ, I was a changed man. My friends knew and I knew that God had begun doing something deep within me that would never end. His hand was now definitely on my life.

Although Christ had delivered me from sin and from alcohol, for about a year I still clung to one habit I couldn't seem to break, smoking. One day a minister told my pastor, "If Lambert didn't smoke I'd invite him to speak in my church. I'm not going to invite any man who smokes into the Lord's pulpit." My pastor relayed this conversation to me very diplomatically, but it hit home. I knew that smoking was keeping me from accomplishing what God wanted, and the other minister's words stung in my memory the way the salt irritates an open wound.

On one occasion I was giving my testimony at a church in Mississippi when someone ransacked my car. I had three or four packs of cigarettes in the car; I usually left them there when I gave my testimony so that I wouldn't be tempted to light up near the church. After the service, when I couldn't find my cigarettes, I thought I would surely die before I found a store where I could replenish my supply.

One day I was testifying to a group of men about all the Lord had done for me. "Say," said one man, "if God is so powerful, why He can't deliver you from those cigarettes you're always puffing?"

That really cut. I felt two inches tall.

At that time our church was holding a series of revival meetings at which Dr. Bob Barker preached. As he spoke about the power of sin and the much greater power of Christ, I made a promise. I asked the Lord to help me stop my addiction and I resolved that with His help I would never smoke another cigar or a cigarette.

As soon as the service was over I walked out of the church, and automatically put a cigarette in my mouth, and lit it. I took two or three puffs and threw it on the ground; I have never smoked since that night. For the first time in my life, I felt completely clean.

Then I made another promise that has profoundly affected my life. For some time my soul had been far from tranquil. I had a disturbing feeling that God had something special for me to do. I was afraid He might want me to enter the ministry, and this really frightened me. I began fighting the idea for all I was worth. I thought of preachers whose shoes I couldn't possibly picture myself filling, or even wanting to fill. I desired strongly to carve out my own career in the world I knew and loved, the world of selling, trade and business. My inner struggles finally came to a climax at a men's prayer meeting. Our pastor held these meetings every Saturday night in his study, and at one of them I promised the Lord I would go anywhere and do anything in His will.

"Lord," I prayed, "You know how unworthy I am to serve you. But if You will open the doors that I might have the opportunity to witness for You, I will step through those doors to the best of my ability."

When I reached the point of complete surrender where

I could say from the heart, "Lord, I'll go anywhere and do anything," I wasn't fighting any longer. Now I was submitting to God's will as completely as I knew how. Then the doors and avenues of service began to open.

I received an invitation to witness at a Baptist Men's Brotherhood meeting at the First Baptist Church of Atmore, Alabama. Shortly afterward the Kiwanis Club of Robertsdale, where Joe Pope had lived, asked me to speak, and then I was invited to the Eastlawn Baptist Church of Pascagoula, Mississippi and to a meeting of the Christian Business Men of Mobile. Again and again I told of how the Lord had met me by the side of the road, as He met the Apostle Paul on the way to Damascus. I have very little in common with Paul except that we both fell to the ground by the roadside when the Lord made Himself real.

Soon I got a telephone call from the Reverend Fred Brown of Pressley Street Baptist Church in Atmore, Alabama. He told me that his church was planning to have a laymen's revival, and he asked me to bring the messages for the week.

What a request to make of a young Christian! The Lord gave me some messages. One was from Romans 5, on "The Fruits of Justification." I spoke about what God gives those who truly believe—peace, access to God, a spirit of rejoicing, hope amidst troubles, the love of God in our hearts, the Holy Spirit, a living Christ. Other passages of Scripture opened up as I prayed and studied; I was given one on "Positive Promises," another on "Missing Our Calling." Before the week of revival messages came to an end, many men and women of Atmore were converted, and many others testified to the help they had received.

I discovered that the Atmore church had a strong group of men who were concerned for individual souls and prayed for them by name, plus a good program of house-to-house visitation. I'm sure that this had more to do with the way God blessed that week of meetings than what I said, but at the same time I had to realize that God was honoring my testimony.

I became a deacon in my church and president of the Mobile Baptist Brotherhood. This brought me into touch with other men's groups and I became Director of the Seventh District of the Alabama Brotherhood and Vice President of the Alabama Brotherhood.

About two years after my conversion I was invited to join the Gideons. For three years I served as President of the Mobile Camp, and I was invited to speak at the Christian Businessmen's International Conventions twice, at Detroit and at Winnipeg. I have spoken at various banquets of the Christian Businessmen's Committee International, in many different parts of the United States. I have participated in many lay crusades of the CBMC and the Baptist Brotherhood.

One night at a city-wide revival in the Mobile auditorium, I had the pleasure of introducing Dr. W. A. Criswell, pastor of the the world's largest Baptist church, First Baptist of Dallas, Texas. Later one man wrote me that a friend from Ohio told him he had never before heard a public official express his Christian belief. "What a change," he wrote, "in our city, state, federal and international relationships, if we had more public figures seeking divine guidance in their lives, rather than attempting to make decisions independently of God."

After another meeting the president of a railroad wrote, "I want you to know how much your witness means to me." I received a letter from Dr. Lee Roberson after I spoke in his great church, "Your testimony brought blessing to all of us." Hudson Baggett, editor of the *Alabama Baptist*, wrote me: "I am extremely grateful that we have men like you in places of leadership, both in the church and in the government." I also treasure a letter from Dr. Criswell in which he said, "Without doubt you are the finest Christian civic leader I have ever seen. I thank God for every remembrance of you." I am grateful for the honor of being elected the first vice president of the 823,00 member Alabama State Baptist Convention.

I have had the honor of speaking at Moody Bible Institute. In 1968 I received an invitation to take part in an evangelistic campaign in the Philippines. I had to decline this as I could not be away from Mobile at the time, but God has been abundantly faithful in opening countless doors of opportunity in witnessing, once I had given him one hundred percent of my life. I am sure that I cannot measure up to all that has been said about me, but I am even more sure that God is able to do more than I, or any other man or woman committed to Him, can ask.

The Lord times everything perfectly. Since I was elected city commissioner, I still get many invitations to speak and to give my testimony, but few of them are for week-long meetings, which I could no longer accept. But in politics my opportunities to witness have expanded a hundredfold. I now have countless opportunities to witness, and a great many people come to my office for counsel and help. Sometimes they confide in me talking about things they wouldn't even tell their own pastors. One woman, an attractive middle-aged person who looked much younger, said that she didn't know anyone else to go to with her problem. She told me that her husband was a minister who had left her for another younger woman. She said her husband had been a real witness for the Lord, and now, whenever she went to church, she wondered if the minister could be like her husband—his life the reverse of his sermons. She was very troubled about this. I explained to her that everyone is tempted and has his own weaknesses, but that we should not judge everyone on the basis of what one person does.

Another lady, who made an appointment to see me, told me that she was in love with a friend of mine who is married and has three children. She, too, professed to be a Christian, although she seemed to feel that falling in love with my friend made everything all right. I suppose she hoped I would help her get him away from his family. She had come to Alabama from another state and I helped her to decide that her best course would be to go back there and leave my friend alone. This she did, and two marriages were saved, for she was married also.

An insurance salesman walked into my office and picked up the red leather Bible I keep there; tears were rolling down his cheeks. He put his cigarette in the ash tray and said,

"You wouldn't believe me, would you, if I told you I'm an ordained preacher?"

"No, John, I have no reason to believe that."

"I was, but now I'm the most miserable man on the face of the earth. I got away from God when things came into my life that I shouldn't have let in. Finally I got so desperate I left the ministry. Now I'm making a good living selling insurance, but I'm almost too miserable to live."

A few weeks later I was privileged to speak at a Baptist men's fellowship meeting at a church where this man was a member. At the close of the service he came forward and re-committed his life to God. He told his pastor, "Now I'm coming back to the Lord." I talked to this man just recently and he told me how good he feels now that the burden of sin is gone.

I have quite a few contacts with alcoholics. One pastor told me that his father was an alcoholic and he wanted me to help him. I talked to the man, but I honestly don't know what results this may have. I do know that many of these men listen carefully to me because they know that I, too was a helpless victim of drink until the Lord rescued me.

One day an old man wandered into my office with alcohol on his breath. He told me his name and his age—eighty-three. "Sir," I said, "you've lived quite a few years, but you won't live forever. What will you do then?" I tried to get him to trust the Lord. Only a few days later he died. I am thankful I was able to witness to him first.

Another man came in, very depressed and in a financial bind. He asked me to pray for him. I said, "Let's have prayer right now," and we prayed in my office. Now he testifies that this helped him over a major crisis.

A veteran who came to see me had a metal plate in his head. Although he was slow of speech, he seemed to have a good mind. He asked me for money, and he was successful in getting ten dollars out of me, in one of the few cases when I have ever done anything like this. Usually, of course, it's very unwise to lend or give money to the many people who ask for it, but this veteran said, "I've come to you because I believe you're a Christian, and I don't have anyone to go to. I have to get to the Veterans' Hospital at Gulfport and I need ten dollars for a bus ticket."

I questioned the young man about his spiritual condition.He had been a church member before he was wounded, but afterward he had become resentful and had strayed from God. I had a good opportunity to talk to him for about thirty minutes as to what the Lord could do for him. Then I handed him a ten-dollar bill. He said, "I'll be back here in sixty days with the money."

After that I forgot about my loan, but sure enough, in about two months the veteran walked in with the ten dollars. He thanked me for two things—lending him the money and talking to him about his spiritual condition. Only eternity will tell, I suppose, what that conversation accomplished.

At one time three news men interviewed me on a television program with a format like "Face the Nation." One of them asked me if my Christian conviction didn't interfere with my political decisions. Right there I had the opportunity to show this man, and the thousands of viewers, that a Christian tries to let everything he does center around Christ. Rather than *interfere* with my decisions, my Christian experience helps me *make* decisions.

I also appeared on the television program "The Story," conducted by the Evangelist Ford Philpot, and after that interview I received letters about it from all over the United States. One man in Maine called his father who lives in Mobile, to say he saw me give my testimony. The Lord has wonderfully blessed these opportunities to witness.

All this boils down to one thing. To be used effectively by the Lord in politics, or anything else, you have to be clean. God tells us definitely, "Be ye clean, that bear the vessels of the Lord" (Isaiah 52:11). "Who shall ascend into the hill of the Lord? or who shall stand in his holy place? He that hath clean hands and a pure heart" (Psalm 24:3,4). "Wherefore come out from among them and be ye separate, saith the Lord, and touch not the unclean thing" (II Corinthians 6:17). When one is in daily contact with the world, it's awfully easy to tough the things that are not clean. Often you come to a place where there's a lot of pressure; you aren't sure what decision to make and you need help. Then there are those borderline cases where something is not really wrong, but it's not really right either, and the temptation is great to slip over the line and do wrong. I need a lot of prayer. I have to pray constantly, asking God to lead and guide and keep me from evil. I have to keep asking, "What would Christ do in this matter?"

Many times I close my office door, get down on my knees and ask God for wisdom. I have to. The people outside the door have no idea what's going on, but I'm praying. I don't ever want to embarrass God, or the people who have put so much confidence in me. I'm a human being and I know how fallible I am, but I would feel like dying if I slipped morally and embarrassed others as a result. I know from experience that when I get too close to the things that are unclean, I find myself getting away from God, and I have to talk to Him until everything is straightened out.

Another thing that makes it tough for a man in public office is the danger of showing any favoritism. I do a lot of traveling to speak on weekends. There is a Christian businessman who has offered to take me anywhere I want to go in his beautifully equipped private airplane. Suppose I accepted this man's generous offer. He has an important position in a concern that does business with many municipalities as well as the state and federal government. The day might well come when I would be sitting across the desk from him to do business, using the tax money of 233,000 persons. It would be most difficult to avoid either showing partiality to this man in some way, or seeming to show it. So, tempting as his offer is, and in as much as both my friend and I want to be completely honest, I don't dare accept.

Then, too, there are gifts. People often want to send me

expensive presents and large gift certificates. I can't accept these, either, for I must not be obligated in any way to anyone with whom I may be concerned as a public official.

Most people of the type who try to offer bribes know better than to approach me. Still, there occasionally have been a few such attempts. When one came came into my office to offer me a deal, I pushed back my chair and stood up so fast that he knew he had said the wrong thing. "Man," I said, "don't ever come back with a proposition like that."

Many men go into politics with good intentions. Often they are nominal church membrs only, not really anchored fast to Christ. Such men can get caught in situations which lead to their downfall. I do not say this boastfully, for the Scripture warns, "Wherefore let him that thinketh he standeth take heed lest he fall" (1 Corinthians 10:12). Anyone who plays with mud is bound to get spattered with it. One little deal can lead to another until a man is caught in a hopeless web of evil. It is possible to make promises you can't fulfill until you are swamped. Then you may be tempted to make more promises to get out of a tight spot, but this can easily lead into a worse corner. Some men get so entangled in this way that they can't get out. They may then be driven to drink, to suicide, to crime or even to insanity.

I find that if I tell the truth, I don't have to worry tomorrow morning about what I said today or yesterday or last week or last year. Before I became a Christian I often got into some situations that had me wracking my brains trying to remember what I had said. I'd try to remember what kind of deal or proposition I had offered to a customer, or to someone my customer knew or might hear about. It ws quite a strain! I would stretch the truth, misrepresent

106

things, or do almost anything to make a sale. Now I no longer have to go through all that mental anguish. I have found that simply by always sticking to the truth, and by never saying anything to be ashamed of, I avoid all kinds of needless worries.

People sometimes come to me after I have given a message and say, "You ought to be a preacher instead of a politician." I don't agree. I am sure I'm exactly where God wants me to be. He has put everything together like a giant puzzle, fitting each piece into the right place as He wants it, and I see His will being done. Things such as have happened in my life just don't happen without a purpose.

Luther Youngdahl once spoke, at a Washington prayer breakfast, of a conversation he had with his mother when she was in the hospital. He was then an ambitious young man and he told his mother of his hopes of winning an election for district judge. She replied, "Son, I know you will win the election. But I want you always to remember that winning elections is not as important as winning souls for Jesus Christ."

I agree completely with her, as Judge Youngdahl did. But I also agree with what this outstanding Christian leader told a church convention in 1960:

"The politician, the worker, the professional man and the merchant are also God's ministers, and their places to witness and ministry are in the market place, the shops, and in public affairs. . . . The world and its thought have not been sufficiently influenced by Christian testimony. The demand of the hour is that the voice of the church will penetrate far more into the current scene. Laymen must be courageous in speaking out no matter what the cost or risk, on issues and problems which intimately concern the men of ourtime."

To be an effective influence for Christ, a person must be filled with the Holy Spirit. Many people figuratively freeze when mention is made of the filling of the Spirit. So much is misundertood about His work, but the Bible teaches that once a sinner is born again, the Holy Spirit comes into his heart. "Now if any man have not the Spirit of Christ, he is none of his," (Romans 8:9). Every Christian has the Holy Spirit, but few Christians experience the filling of the Spirit, or control by the Holy Spirit. Most of us keep Him boxed up in our hearts. We suppress Him. We never let Him really have His way. When we die to ourselves and crucify the old sinful nature, we decrease and we let His increase. The Holy Spirit must control our feelings, direct our wills and equip us for service.

I'm convinced that I can do more for the Lord right where I am than anywhere else. However, I must add most sincerely that if I felt that God wanted me to be a pastor, a missionary or something else, I would resign my position at City Hall and go where He led.

I may be originally from the cotton patch but God has given me enough sense to know that I'm where I am today not because of *my* brains or ability, but because God has performed miracles.

It's unbelievable what He has done in my life. Sometimes I have to pinch myself to see if this is really me. I thank the Lord constantly that he is never content with less than one hundred percent.

12

A Layman Looks at the Church

SOME TIME AGO I saw a newspaper article headed, CALI-FORNIA CHURCH GOES MODERN. Describing a certain church's new social hall, it said, "The Place is an off-beat coffee house alternating provocative films with wild dances." Recently a church in Wisconsin held a "eucharistic dance" at which the young people recited the words, "It is a time of tension and despair for riots are at the door." Later one woman said of the service, "I think it was disgraceful." At a church party in Missouri young people smashed a car with a sledge hammer while others scribbled such slogans as FREE SEX AND SODA POP on the walls and picketers carried signs reading, CHURCH UNFAIR TO JESUS. As part of its worship service a New York church presented part of a play about an alcoholic birthday party for homosexuals, after which the minister said, "Variations of sex are not sin." A midwestern church presented the play *Paradise Now* at which members of the audience took off their clothing and joined the performers in a flesh pile as they called for a sexual revolution.

A church in the East used go-go girls to attract a crowd while still another gave trading stamps to stimulate Sunday school attendance. One woman wrote a noted evangelist, "I attend a church here and I am concerned about its worldliness. Just recently it observed the Lord's Supper. However, the minister served water to represent the Lord's blood and salty crackers to represent His body. And while 'Communion' was going on, he played a jazz record with the 'Batman' theme."

A survey reported by a national news weekly indicated that sixty-four percent of the members of one church seldom or never pray, ninety percent do not believe in life after death, and less than three percent believe that God is a supernatural being. The report said, "Most of them deny the major tenets of Christianity." Another large denomination published a book which said, "No longer is it legitimately possible for the Christian to claim with the Old Testament psalmist, The fool hath said in his heart, There is no God.'"

Even among conservative churches, however, there is often a form of godliness without power. In this chapter, I would like to share my views as a layman who expects certain things of the church and wants to do what he can to help it fulfill its great purpose.

In his first epistle, the Apostle Peter wrote as an elder to other elders or spiritual guides of the church, "Feed the flock of God" (5:2). The first and primary responsibility of a shepherd is to feed his sheep. The ancient shepherd made every effort to provide for his flock the best grazing area he could find. Nothing could stop him from searching out the most fertile valleys to provide his sheep with luscious fields of grass.

The church is the flock of God. The primary responsibility of the leaders and pastors of the various churches is not to be administrators, promoters or organizers, although these things may be important and necessary, but to feed the flock. I am afraid that time is often spent on building programs while the sheep go hungry. Too little time is spent in prayer while the flock is dying of malnutrition. Too little time is spent on sermon preparation while the sheep become weak for lack of spiritual food.

One of the greatest needs in this country today is the need for spiritual food. Millions of people make an effort to go to church and often all they hear are a few empty prayers, a song or two communicating no spiritual solace, twenty minutes of announcements, and someone's opinion of what is wrong with the world. They leave, after an hour of what should have been an hour of spiritual feeding, hungry and empty, totally unprepared to face this sin-infested world and the tempter who goes about like a roaring lion seeking whom he may devour. And day after day literally thousands of God's sheep are indeed devoured by the enemy because they sought nourishment and found none. As one who lives out in the world, I say that it is impossible for the people of God to live as He wants us to if we are not spiritually nourished.

The people in the churches are dying for want of the Word of God—not entertainment, not the latest news or sociological opinions, not jokes or announcements but the message of the Lord. If a pastor is to do what God expects of him and what his laymen expect of him, he cannot come before his people unprepared. He must open the Word of God and feed his people with nourishment for their souls. I asked a number of laymen from different denominations to outline what they expected of their ministers. Each one expressed a great need in his life for victory over sin and for strength to live in a Christlike way, and each insisted that the minister preach the Word and feed the flock.

Two-thirds of the prisoners in Alabama's prisons and penitentiaries are Baptists. Throughout our nation a large number of church members are locked behind bars for various crimes. Once these men made a profession of faith in Christ. Once they were baptized. Once they sat under someone's preaching. Was it empty? Was it filled with idle words? Was the flock really fed? Evidently not! As people come to me in Mobile's City Hall with so many serious spiritual problems, I am convinced that many of their difficulties would not exist if they had been given the proper spiritual food in their churches. It is the Word of God that men and women need desperately, in order to resist evil and live for Christ.

My activity in lay evangelistic work in my own denomination and in interdenominational areas puts me in touch with many ministers, and I value the close friendship I have with many of God's choice servants. Their confidence in me is greatly appreciated; on many occasions pastors have consulted me about personal problems of their own and of their congregations. However, more ministers than I would like to remember have asked me to put their names before certain pulpit committees. Some of them seemed more concerned about getting their names before another flock than about feeding the flock that God had given them. I know, too, that after a man has prayed to be moved out of what he thought was an unbearable situation, he may find himself in an even worse predicament. The grass is not always greener on the other side of the fence! It is also my impression that too many pastors are out feeding other flocks to the neglect of their own. Most laymen are glad when their ministers can help other congregations, but no pastor can feed his own sheep properly when he is away Sunday after Sunday, even though he is conducting revivals somewhere else. His first concern is to his own people. Saint Peter admonished, "Feed the flock of God which is among you."

The Apostle also told the pastors to whom he wrote to take ". . . the oversight thereof, not by constraint, but willingly; not for filthy lucre, but of a ready mind; Neither as being lords over God's heritage, but being examples to the flock." The shepherd of the ancient world not only provided food for his flock, but he tended it, nurturing, guiding and guarding the sheep. He knew their bleats and they knew his voice. He was constantly on watch; not one wolf could come near, nor one sheep go astray, without his knowledge. A good shepherd is a good overseer. The people of God need pastors who know their needs, who can detect unhappiness and false smiles and can look with sympathy into their problems. A good overseer knows what is going on among those with whom he works. He knows their weaknesses, their faults, their good points and their bad qualities.

This oversight must not be done out of a sense of duty alone, but out of love and compassion, willingly, and as God would have it done.

Miss Bertha Smith, a Southern Baptist Missionary to the Orient for forty-two years, relates an incident that happened during the months that preceeded the great Shantung Revival. Many of the missionaries had a humbling experience when they were led to confess to the Chinese that they worked with them out of a sense of obligation rather than out of a heart of love, compassion and patience. A revival came. I believe that today if some of our spiritual leaders were to confess their sins and get them forgiven up to date, so to speak, we would have a revival such as this world has never known.

Spiritual overseeing should also be done with a ready mind. God's flock must be tended cheerfully and eagerly. Some pastors have told me that their work was no longer a work of joy but one of drudgery; to minister was no longer a pleasant task but one to be dreaded. No doubt

113

some of this is due to overwork, because many pastors today are too involved in teaching Sunday school classes, heading all committees and other activities which should be done by the lay people. Now I realize, too, that some of us laymen are hard to shepherd, and I know that some of us require a lot of time; but let me say that no matter what the problems may be, when the work of feeding the flock of God has become a dread or a drudgery, then it is not as God would want it.

In the survey I mentioned earlier in this chapter, each participant expected his pastor to be an example, just as the Apostle Peter says that he should be. In each case the participant spelled out specific areas in which he felt the example should be set. One was in *Christian living.* More impact is made on a community by the way a minister acts out of the pulpit than by what he says from behind it. I have heard waitresses, people who operate golf courses, and others who are in contact with certain ministers say of them, "You would never know he's a preacher, would you?" This is an indictment of the Christian minister. When he is in a hurry to make some visits, and the clerk in the grocery store needs a little extra time to check out an error in the bill, when he must be at the hospital by eight-thirty and the service station attendant is a little slow in filling the gas tank, when Sister Smith dresses him down for something he should have done or not done, the man of Christ must remember that he is an example.

Another area is *sincerity.* A philosophy of "Do as I say, not as I do," doesn't work. No minister can expect his people to do something that he would not do. People can tell if a man is sincere and means what he says.

Third, the participants in the survey listed *honesty.* Probably the number is very small, but unfortunately there are ministers who have been atrocious examples in their communities by failing in this important area, as in failing to pay their debts. I have known personally some pastors who have written worthless checks. It is shameful when a banker remarks that preachers are the worst credit risks he knows.

Almost every person surveyed, expected his pastor to keep in confidence those problems and burdens about which he was consulted. *Reliance* is surely an important aspect of being a good example to the flock. A person should be able to depend on his pastor not to reveal anything told him in confidence, even to fellow pastors.

Ministers should be an example in *appearance*. No one expects a pastor or his family to dress in sackcloth, but neither need the pastor don the latest Hollywood styles. I have seen evangelists with such loud coats they looked more like circus clowns than ministers, and clergymen's wives and daughters who dressed almost the way you might expect Raquel Welch to be garbed to entertain the troops in Vietnam. Thank God these are few and far between, but improper dress is something that all Christians should guard against.

I believe a layman can expect ministers of the gospel to be an example in many ways—in dependability, community activity and much else—but above all they should excel in *faithfulness*. As citizens we are no stronger than our spiritual leaders. If they are faithful to God and their calling, ours will be a better nation and a better world.

Still, I would not wish to give the impression that ministers bear all responsibility for the condition of the church. In many instances the example, the testimony and the influence of the layman is more effective than that of the minister. In Acts 6:10 we read of a man with no seminary

115

training, a layman and deacon named Stephen: "They were not able to resist the wisdom and the spirit by which he spake." Why was this man's witness so powerful? First, because *he was a man of faith.* When the first deacons were selected, the work of the Lord was growing so rapidly that the Apostles needed help. In order to have time for Bible study, prayer and preaching, the Apostles agreed to choose seven men to help them. "And they chose Stephen, a man full of faith" (Acts 6:5). Stephen had had a vital experience with Christ. When he spoke of his Saviour he was sure of himself; he could speak personally about Christ because he had had a personal experience with Him. He had been an eyewitness of the Lord's saving power. Stephen knew what he was talking about and those who heard him *knew* that he knew what he was talking about. I could tell you about Niagara Falls, but I know a man who could tell you about that natural wonder in such a manner that you could almost feel the water spraying your face and hear the thundering roar of millions of gallons of water rushing over the brink to the rocks below. The difference is that he has been there and I haven't. The same thing is true about Christ and salvation. One must experience His power in a very personal way before he can effectively tell someone else about Him.

Stephen the deacon was also a man of ". . . honest report . . ." (Acts 6:3). *He was faithful toward his fellow men.* He could be trusted; his word was his bond; his neighbors could count on him. Well spoken of and reliable, he was a person believed by his friends and acquaintances. A man cannot engage in shady business deals or crooked politics through the week and lead someone to Christ on visitation night. He cannot be unfaithful in his relationships and be a Christian influence in his community. If we Christians would practice what we preach for just one week, the world would never be the same again. If we did this for seven days of every week of every year, untold millions would come to know Christ.

Some time ago, while waiting to see a certain business-man, I overheard a conversation. One salesman had the floor, telling dirty jokes and relating how bad he felt from too many drinks the night before. My time came to see the buyer and I went on about my business. A few days later I went to a church to fill a speaking engagement at a men's banquet. The first man I saw when I walked into the fellow-ship hall was this salesman. To say he was embarrassed would be an understatement. When he saw me, he turned every color in the rainbow. You may imagine my disap-pointment when I learned that he was secretary of the group. Here was a man preaching one thing at church and practicing another out in the business world.

We must practice what we preach! If Jesus is worth having for an hour on Sunday, He is worth having and living for every day of the week. It is imperative that we be of honest report and faithful toward our fellow man, if our witness is to count for Christ.

Stephen's witness was powerful because *he was a fearless man*. Upon hearing his witness many were stirred and convicted. Some received his message and accepted his Saviour. Some rejected and resented his message, persuad-ing others to make false accusations agains him. They brought him before the council of the Sanhedrin.

There, instead of hanging his head in shame, or perhaps denying Christ as others had done, Stephen stood steadfast and immovable for Christ, preaching, in his hour of trial, one of the greatest sermons recorded in God's Word. In this instance he showed his accusers that they had not only persecuted the prophets, but had crucified the Son of God.

"When they heard these things, they were cut to the heart, and they gnashed on him with their teeth" (Acts 7:54).

They took him out to stone him and even as they hurled the stones which would take his life this great man of God stood fearlessly for Christ. If our testimony is to count for Christ, we also must stand without fear. "If God be for us, who can be against us?" (Romans 8:31). Men must stand for Christ in offices, in factories, and on the job all over this world.

What the world needs is men of courage. Too many mealy-mouths and too many tight-mouth Christians bring shame to Christ's name. Let us be true and unashamed in every area of life. Paul said, "I am not ashamed of the gospel" (Romans 1:16). Why? Because "it is the power of God unto salvation to everyone that believeth, to the Jew first and also to the Greek" (Romans 1:16). God help us to stand steadfast and to proclaim the gospel.

The fourth thing that made Stephen's testimony so powerful was that *he was full of the Spirit.' "And they chose Stephen, a man full of . . . the Holy Ghost" (Acts 6:5).* The *Amplified New Testament* says that he was full of and controlled by the Holy Spirit of God. In the previous chapter I wrote of the filling of the Spirit. The layman Stephen is an example of what every member of the church of Christ should be. Christ promised, "But ye shall receive power, after that the Holy Ghost is come upon you: and ye shall be witnesses unto me both in Jerusalem, and in all Judaea, and in Samaria, and unto the uttermost part of the earth" (Acts 1:8).

Luther W. Youngdahl told a high school graduating class: "It is my earnest conviction that the world is in its present predicament because of our unwillingness to really accept Christ. . . . We haven't been willing to pay the price of living the Christian way of life. Too many people profess to be followers of Christian principles but give only lip service. This is a dangerous attitude at a time when the Christian world faces its most crucial test. The call, then, is for a fiery, zealous devotion to Jesus. There was never a time when the ardor of true discipleship was more needed than now. . . . If the world is changed for the better, it is going to be done by each of us taking the slow, hard road of discipline and unselfishness. The great power of Christianity comes only as one person, and another person, and another is willing to put the teachings of Christ into actual practice in daily life."

When the members and ministers of the church do that, the church of Chist will be the most powerful agency in the world to meet human needs and bring glory to God.

13

To Turn the Tide

WE LIVE IN A time of unprecedented peril. Millions of American citizens who seem to think that the world owes them a living, look for government handouts and receive them, never grateful and constantly critical. A recent article in the *Mobile Press* states that the National Commission on Technology, Automation and Economic Progress has recommended to the president that every American family be guaranteed a minimum annual income of three thousand dollars. This could affect more than thirty-five million Americans and cost as much as twenty billion dollars a year. The average working person already spends two and one-half hours out of every eight simply paying hs present taxes—local, state and federal. How much farther can such trends expand?

Today a large part of the world is under communist control. In our own country, men and women who bask in the sunshine of our freedoms are doing everything they can to destroy the very foundations on which these freedoms have been established. It is a time of riots in the streets, on the campuses and throughout the land. Recently in Georgia, five lawbreakers stole seventy-five dollars from the collection plates of a Negro church and then took two of the choir girls into the woods, raped them and left them there. Not long ago in the Netherlands, a priest married a homosexual couple. In a travesty of the marriage ceremony, these two men pledged to each other their mutual fidelity.

Our generation faces a sex explosion. Free love is the answer to every problem, in the view of many. A common attitude is love today, pay tomorrow. On the campuses, students are demanding, and getting, absolute freedom in this area. Not long ago I obtained from Grady Wilson of the Billy Graham Association a copy of the membership application of the Sexual Freedom Forum. It was being passed out by eighteen-year-olds at the Berkeley campus of the University of California and it contained such questions as these:

Are you interested in:

1. Nude parties?
2. Clothed parties?
3. Nude bathing?
4. Eroticism classes?
5. Sexuality discussion groups?
6. Exchanging photographs?
7. Mate swapping?

A Berkeley campus newspaper contains these advertisements:

Male student needs female to share his furnished apartment.

Gentle, vital, highly creative man would love to be contacted by unpossessive sensual woman.

Man 32 wishes to share 3 large bedrooms. Completely remodeled home. FM, stereo, color TV. Women only.

Today wife-swapping, wholesale adultery, and forms of

121

sexual perversion are so common that they receive little attention. Our high schools are filled with non-virgin clubs, and girls who do not go along with the crowd are called freaks and squares. One of our large cities spends thousands of dollars annually for day care centers for the children of high school girls; recently there were 1,876 such girls expecting babies who would be born out of wedlock, most of them between the ages of fifteen and sixteen. On some college campuses contraceptive pills are available to anyone.

The columnist Patricia Young recently wrote:

> Just for the record—and without apology—I AM A REACTIONARY! I react to sin and sadism, riots and revolution, gutlessness and godlessness! I react to hedonism and humanism, to philosophies and sophistries which seek to destroy those values which made this country great; which fashioned the fabric of civilized mankind.
>
> I react to dancing the permissive polka with those who'd whirl me all the way to hell while whispering that God is dead and the devil a myth; to those ministers who'd convert my house of worship into a hootenanny hall or pollitical forum. I react to the emasculation of my faith in the name of humanistic togetherness; to my love for the Holy Bible, my loyalty to the flag and my esteem for the police. . . I react to the glorification of welfarism over work; pot over pink lemonade; the pill over purity; demonstration over dedication; desire over discipline; nihilism over nobility; selfishness over sacrifice; hauteur over humility; "rights" over right.

> *Presbyterian Layman*, January,1969

In his second epistle to Timothy the Apostle Paul stated

that perilous times were coming. The days will be diffi-cult,he predicted, and the times will be grievous; men will be lovers of their own selves, covetous, boastful, proud, blasphemous, disobedient, unthankful, and unholy. They will be truce-breakers, false accusers, incontinent, fierce, despisers of those who are good, traitors, lovers of pleasure more than lovers of God, having a form of godliness but denying the power thereof. It is my sincere belief that we have now entered the days Paul described.

Our generation is caught in a tide of no return, unless we halt the destructive influences that are crumbling our na-tion's most sacred possessions before our eyes. There are enough people speaking up today for socialism, commu-nism, revolution, smut, sex perversion, and every kind of license—all in the name of liberty. It's time more Chris-tians spoke up for what is right, and time we did something positive to halt the tide of evil that seems to be rolling with increasing force throughout the world. I know what God can do through individuals committed to His will, and I want to encourage more people to become ". . . labourers together with God," as Paul expressed it in I Corinthians 3:9. I believe that there are definite steps we can take to turn the tide and halt the rush toward chaos. The first sounds simple, although it is one of the most basic things we can ever do. It is *remembrance.*

We need to remember God's blessings. Our Creator has truly blessed our land. It was He who led holy men to this country in the 1600's, who believed that individuals should be free to worship God as they saw fit. It was God who inspired the pilgrim fathers to enter into the Mayflower Compact which recognizes the glory of God as the su-preme purpose in forming a new political entity. It was God who raised up Washington, Jefferson, Adams, Franklin, and thousands like them to chip this nation out of the wilderness piece by piece, mile by mile, and to carve out the land of the free and the home of the brave. It was God who made ours the wealthiest nation of all time. He permitted our people, with only six percent of the world's population, to acquire fifty percent of the world's wealth, twenty-nine percent of its railroads, sixty-eight percent of its automobiles, fifty-one percent of its trucks, and fifty-two percent of its radios; He enabled us to produce forty-one percent of the petroleum and twenty-nine percent of the coal in the whole world. God has let us become the greatest power on earth. Let us thank Him continually for His hand of blessing upon our country.

We must also remember God's wrath. The Creator is no soft, foolishly sentimental grandparent; in the words of Scripture He is "a jealous God." He commands, ". . . have no other gods before me." He warns, "The wicked shall be turned into hell, and all the nations that forget God" (Psalm 9:17). A nation that forgets God is in trouble, and I'm afraid we in America have forgotten Him.

How do we stand morally? American pornography floods and scandalizes the world. The United States has more "B girls" than college girls, more bars than churches, and more taverns and liquor stores than grocery stores. Arrests are at an all-time high, and the amount of crime is skyrocketing in every part of our country.

I am afraid we have forgotten God in the business world. Much advertising is so false that no one believes it. Unethical business practices and disregard for the Lord's day are widespread.

In the political world, faith is often conspicuous by its absence. Some say that religion and politics do not mix. I say that what we need is godly men to let their Christian influence count in places of leadership. In this country's earlier years, our statesmen were men of high Christian character, leaders in their churches, and they didn't do too badly in guiding our destiny. They sought God's guidance in the decisions that affected the welfare of their people. Today too many men and women are seeking to take God out of every phase of public life. Our national capital has streets lined with bars and taverns, and its sales of alcohol are higher per capita than in any other city. What does this say for the heart of our nation?

I fear that we have forgotten God in the area of education. In many institutions of higher learning God is mocked, and in our public schools simple prayers and the reading of theBible have been prohibited. There is pressure in some school systems to take the words *under God* out of the pledge to the flag.

In these days of declining faith in God, men are worshiping the god of Prosperity, the god of Power, the god of Popularity, and the god of Pleasure, but the true God is a jealous God, and He cannot honor those who dishonor Him. We need to remember both His blessings and His wrath.

Today distress and perplexity abound, just as the Bible predicted they would in the last days. What is the answer? Is it church membership? The United States already has one hundred and twenty million church members. I believe that Christians ought to join and support the churches, but I know from my own experience that church membership alone is not the answer. I myself was a church member for fifteen years before I had peace in my heart. There are thousands of church members marching in the streets, breaking down law and order, committing crime, and even shedding blood and taking life. The answer to our deepest problems is not registration of names in a church but regeneration of individuals.

The Bible describes our needs and our times with vivid accuracy. It says there is no peace in the hearts of the wicked; we are like a troubled sea, always tossing and turning, and casting up mire. We have evil hearts. We have sinned and fallen short of the glory of God; there is none that doeth good. The troubled sea of life can be calmed only by the Prince of Peace. Jesus Christ, the Son of God, can bring real peace to the heart. He invites, "Come unto me, all ye that labour and are heavy laden, and I will give you rest" (Matthew 11:28). When we turn to Him in simple childlike faith, realizing our need for Him and asking Him to come into our hearts, a miracle takes place. We are reborn, regenerated. We become children of God and followers of Christ. Then and then only do we have in our hearts the peace that passes understanding. When men have the peace of God in their hearts they can live in peace together.

This applies to our civic leaders. Let me say with love and humility, and yet with deep conviction, that the political leader cannot be the kind of leader he should be until he is born from above. I would hate to know I had to serve as city commissioner and Mayor of Mobile if I were not a Christian, or if I did not have Christ to help me. Many times I call on Him. He is always there—through every situation, every predicament, every temptation. A personal relationship with Jesus Christ is imperative!

The third thing we need to turn the tide of evil is rededication. America must mend its ways, tear down its altars to other gods and return to the Almighty. We must reestablish family altars, brush the dust off our Bibles and rededicate ourselves to God, His Book and His principles.

We must determine to live for Him no matter what the price.

We also need rededication to the principles of true Americanism. The late President John F. Kennedy said, "America has become become a land of spectators." Hundreds of thousands of spectators gather each fall to watch twenty-two men play football, and literally millions watch the sport on television. Every summer enormous crowds spend a great deal of money and time viewing eighteen men playing baseball.

We are spectators in more than sports. Year after year two hundred million American spectators sit back and watch while a few people run the government. Apathy and indifference are on every hand. It is time for Americans to leave the sidelines of unconcern and get into the game as participants in public life. We must stand for our freedoms, return to the principles on which our nation was founded, and put loyalty to America above personal gain, selfish interests, personalities and party politics.

In the past we Christians have been so careful to maintain the separation of church and state that we have separated ourselves from civic responsibility. Some citizens do not even take the trouble to vote. This is tragic. Christans must involve themselves in community affairs and national and world affairs. If this country is going to be saved, God's people will have to come to the forefront, roll up their sleeves and get busy. There are far too many citizens who do not want to get mixed up in politics, but politics in itself is neither good nor evil. It's what we make of the science of government that makes the difference. Public service involves humanity, and Jesus was concerned about both the physical and the spiritual needs of people. As followers of Christ today, it is vital for us to be concerned about our fellow men and involved in their search for a just and satisfying life.

With the help of God, the tide can be turned and the future of America can be great.